The Charism of
Priestly Celibacy

The Charism of Priestly Celibacy

BIBLICAL, THEOLOGICAL, and PASTORAL REFLECTIONS

Edited by John C. Cavadini
Institute for Church Life

ave maria press AmP notre dame, indiana

Paperback: ISBN-10 1-59471-361-8   ISBN-13 978-1-59471-361-3

E-book: ISBN-10 1-59471-362-6   ISBN-13 978-1-59471-362-0

Cover image © Nevena Tsvetanova / Alamy.

Cover and text design by John R. Carson.

Printed and bound in the United States of America.

Library of Congress Cataloging-in-Publication Data
The charism of priestly celibacy : Biblical, theological, and pastoral reflections / edited by John C. Cavadini.
    p. cm.
"The Institute for Church Life."
Includes bibliographical references.
ISBN 978-1-59471-361-3 (pbk.) -- ISBN 1-59471-361-8 (pbk.)
1. Celibacy. 2. Catholic Church--Clergy. I. Cavadini, John C. II. University of Notre Dame. Institute for Church Life.

BX1912.85.C46 2012
253'.252--dc23

2012022132

Contents

Introduction

John C. Cavadini, PhD

What is the meaning of priestly celibacy? It is sometimes explained that celibacy is a "discipline" that the Roman Catholic Church observes, and yet that explanation can itself be misleading. Is celibacy simply a practical discipline, providing for increased availability of the priest? Is it simply an ascetic practice that is meant to provide a kind of spiritual training appropriate for all Christians, even if not all Christians can train at such a "high" level? Or is there more to the idea of priestly celibacy? Is there an ideal here, one that grows out of the very theology of the priesthood, connected to it by a fittingness and a congruency, if not an absolute necessity, that has been present in some way from the earliest days and discerned more and more deeply through the ages of reflecting on her own mission and identity? It is the latter that is the premise for this volume of essays. By exploring the history and theology of priestly celibacy, the essays in this volume hope to contribute to a deeper appreciation of the beauty of this charism, and so to a deeper appreciation of the beauty of priestly life. This volume was undertaken in the conviction that, without prejudice to the practice of other Churches, in reflecting on the charism of priestly celibacy, one will come to a deeper understanding not just of a discipline only extrinsically and accidentally related to the priesthood, but of priestly life itself.

The best theology, we know, is intrinsically pastoral in that it seeks an "understanding" of the faith of the Church in order to build up the one Body by strengthening conviction and awakening a more lively gratitude for the gifts of God that faith believes in. We hope that this volume provides a good example of a conversation which is as irreducibly pastoral as it is theological. The papers modulate in voice, emphasizing at times the more strictly speaking technical and theological, and at times the more strictly speaking homiletic and pastoral. Yet we hope they form one seamless conversation with the goal of providing a more profound contemplation and reception of an ideal that we can sometimes take for granted or else regard as something purely negative, instead seeing in it a particular instance of Christian generosity and love especially appropriate to the pastoral charity of ordained ministry. In this way, we hope this volume will provide a service for those pondering a vocation to priestly life, for those encouraging and advising them, and for those engaged in the education of seminarians. We hope, too, that this volume will be useful for those already ordained who may wish to reflect more deeply on the ideals they have embraced and desire to live them out ever more effectively. In fact we hope the volume can provide an increased understanding of the charism of priestly celibacy for anyone wishing to understand it more fully, or to explain it to others.

The papers in this volume were originally given by participants in a conference jointly sponsored by the USCCB Committee on Doctrine and the Institute for Church Life at the University of Notre Dame. The conference took place February 15–17, 2012, on the campus of the University of Notre Dame. I would like to thank His Eminence Donald Cardinal Wuerl, Chairman of the Committee on Doctrine, for his enthusiastic support of this project from its inception. I would also like to thank Fr. Thomas G. Weinandy, O.F.M. Cap., Executive Director of the Secretariat for Doctrine, with whom I worked closely in the planning and execution of the conference. I would also like to thank Angela Partida, administrative assistant for the Committee on Doctrine, Virginia Nawrocki, administrative assistant for the Institute for Church Life, as well as Jennifer Monahan, Assistant Director of the Institute for Church Life, and Brian Shappell, Business Manager of the Institute for Church Life. The conference was made possible by a grant from the Lilly Endowment under the "Sustaining Pastoral Excellence" initiative, and I would like to express my thanks to Craig Dykstra and to John Wimmer for their generosity and assistance. Finally, I want to thank Bob Hamma of Ave Maria Press for all of his expert assistance. Of course, where I have not taken the good advice of any of these excellent colleagues, the fault is mine alone.

April 16, 2012, Second Monday of the Easter Season,

John C. Cavadini, PhD
McGrath-Cavadini Director
Institute for Church Life

1

Dimensions of Priestly Celibacy

Rev. Raniero Cantalamessa, O.F.M. Cap.

Priestly celibacy has become the topic of numerous debates in the Church today and is often looked at with suspicion and pity outside the Church. In this kind of atmosphere the very word "celibacy" evokes the idea of an unresolved problem, of a "burning" issue, rather than evoking the idea of a freely accepted commitment and a gift of grace. Today, celibacy is not lived out tranquilly, and all its spiritual fruitfulness fails to be realized because of all the fuss around it or perhaps because it is thought that one day—who knows?—Church law about it might change.

What is needed, therefore, is a complete reversal of our mind-set, and this can happen only through renewed contact with the biblical and theological roots of this state of life. We are now living in a social environment in which one can no longer rely on external kinds of protections and the detailed precautions with which traditional asceticism and canon law used to surround the observance of celibacy. The facility of communication and of travel has created a new situation: television, the Internet, advertisements, and newspapers flood our homes with the world and force us to look at it. Maintaining chastity is now entrusted to the individual for the most part and cannot rely on anything except firm personal convictions drawn from the Word of God.

I would like the reflections I was asked to prepare to further this end. The topic assigned to me allows me to speak about ecclesiastical celibacy in completely positive terms, because perfect chastity for the sake of the kingdom was, is, and always will be part of Christ's intentions. I leave to other writers the problematic aspects of historical, canonical, and pastoral issues that are also being addressed.

Mandatory celibacy for priests is one of the many forms that the evangelical proposal of perfect chastity for the kingdom of heaven has taken in the history of the Church. Consequently, we need to begin again from the original text to understand the meaning and value of chastity. That is the reason I will often speak simultaneously of priestly celibacy and consecrated virginity, or the vow of chastity. One text from the Second Vatican Council, *Prefectae caritatis*, summarizes this evangelical value:

> Chastity "for the sake of the kingdom of heaven" (Mt 19:12), which religious profess, must be esteemed as an exceptional gift of grace. It uniquely frees the hearts of men and women (see 1 Cor 7:32–35), so that they become more fervent in love for God and for all humanity. For this reason it is a special symbol of heavenly benefits, and for religious it is a most effective way of dedicating themselves wholeheartedly to the divine service and the works of the apostolate. Thus, for all Christ's faithful, religious recall that wonderful marriage made by God which will be fully manifested in the age to come, and in which the church has Christ alone for her spouse.[1]

This text highlights the various dimensions of celibacy and consecrated virginity explored in this chapter: the prophetic dimension, the apostolic or missionary dimension, and the spousal dimension. To these three dimensions, I will add a fourth one, the charismatic dimension.

PROPHETIC DIMENSION OF PRIESTLY CELIBACY

The prophetic or missionary dimension of celibacy is the one that emerges the most clearly from Christ's saying about those who are eunuchs for the kingdom of heaven:

> The disciples said to him, "If such is the case of a man with his wife [that he cannot divorce her], it is not expedient to marry." But he said to them, "not all men can receive this precept, but only those to whom it is given. For there are eunuchs who have been so from birth, and there are eunuchs who have been made eunuchs by men, and there are eunuchs who have made themselves eunuchs for the sake of the kingdom of heaven. He who is able to receive this, let him receive it. (Mt 19:10–12)

The word "eunuch" was harsh and offensive at that time, as it is for us today. If Jesus uses it in this context, it is probably because his adversaries were accusing him of being a eunuch because he was not married, the same way they accused him of being a glutton, a drunkard, and a friend of publicans. In taking up what his adversaries were saying, however, he conferred a wholly new meaning to that word, a spiritual meaning instead of the physical one. Christian tradition has always understood the word "eunuch" in this text that way, except for the famous case of Origen who, contrary to his habit of explaining everything spiritually, interpreted this passage literally and mutilated himself, paying a high price later for his error.

Jesus established a second state of life in the world, and this text is its "Magna Carta." In fact, before Jesus no state of life comparable to this existed, at least in terms of motivation if not in practice, even among the Essenes. This new state of life does not nullify the alternative state of marriage, but it makes marriage relative. It is analogous to what happens to the idea of a state in the world of politics. Marriage is not abolished, but it becomes relativized by the presence in history of the kingdom of God; it is no longer the absolute and supreme norm for living. Perfect chastity does not require the disavowal of marriage in order for its validity to be recognized. On the contrary, it has no meaning apart from a simultaneous affirmation of marriage. If marriage were something negative, renouncing it would be not a free choice but a duty. It is precisely the institution of this second state of life that now makes marriage itself a "vocation" and not simply a natural obligation.

To understand the inner logic for this new state of life, we need to start with the motive presented by Jesus: "for the sake of the kingdom of heaven." The kingdom of God (which Matthew calls the kingdom "of heaven" according to Jewish custom) has a dual characteristic that theologians today generally express by using two adverbs for time: "already" and "not yet." It is "already" here; it has come and is now present. The kingdom of heaven, Jesus proclaims, is at hand; it is in your midst. But in another sense, the kingdom of heaven has not yet come; it is still on its way, and it is for this reason that Jesus invites us in the "Our Father" to pray, "Thy kingdom come" (Mt 6:10).

Since the kingdom of heaven has already come and in Christ ultimate salvation is already at work in the world, it is possible that some people, called by God, may choose to live, here and now, as people will live in their ultimate state in the kingdom. In the Gospel of Luke, Jesus describes that ultimate state:

> The sons of this age marry and are given in marriage, but those who are accounted worthy to attain to that age and to the resurrection from the dead neither marry nor are given in marriage, for they cannot die any more, because they are equal to angels and are sons of God, being sons of the resurrection. (Lk 20:34–36; see also Mt 22:30)

The *prophetic dimension* of virginity and celibacy for the sake of the kingdom lies precisely in this. This state of life, through its very existence, shows what the ultimate state of human beings will be, and it is destined to last forever. This prophetic state of life, far from being opposed to married people, is instead to their advantage. It reminds them that marriage is holy, beautiful, created by God, and redeemed by Christ. It is an image of the marriage between Christ and the Church, but that is not the whole story. Marriage is a structure tied to this world and is therefore transitory. When people can no longer die, they will no longer need to marry. There will be no need to "complete oneself" with another human being at the time when "God [will] be everything to every one" (1 Cor 15:28).

We know how easy it is to make a good marriage an ideal and the ultimate goal in life, considering its success to be success in life itself. The first thing that suffers from making marriage unduly absolute is marriage itself, which becomes nearly crushed by these disproportionate expectations that can never be fulfilled, and thus it can enter into crisis at the first sign of difficulty. That is why I say that the alternative state of life created by Christ is a help to married people themselves. It frees up marriage and each of the two spouses from the unbearable burden of having to be everything to each other and to take God's place.

In light of this prophetic character of virginity and celibacy, we can understand how misleading and false is the thesis that this state of life is contrary to nature and hinders men and women from being fully themselves, that is, from being a real man or woman. This concern weighs terribly on the minds of young people and is one of the reasons that holds them back the most from responding to a religious or priestly vocation. People do not always take into account that this thesis was established by the founders of modern psychology on the basis of a materialistic and atheistic view of the human being. What psychology has to say on this issue may carry a certain weight for someone who does not believe in the existence of God or in the immortality of the soul, but it has no weight at all for the person who sees human beings from the perspective of faith or at least from something other than a completely materialistic point of view.

Virginity and celibacy do not deny nature but rather fulfill it at a more profound level. To know what a human being is and what is "natural" for a person, human reasoning (especially when influenced by Greek philosophy) has always based itself on its analysis of human *nature* (*physis*), meaning, according to the etymology of "nature," what a person is by *birth*: a *rational animal*.

The Bible does not recognize the concept of nature in this way. According to the Bible, an individual is not only what he or she is determined to be through birth but also what he or she is called to become through the exercise of freedom in obedience to God. To be a human being is a "vocation"! Existential thinking came close to this vision, making freedom and self-determination the meaning of human existence. Unfortunately, many of its representatives (except Søren Kierkegaard who was its founder) eliminated an essential element found in the biblical definition: "in obedience to God." For example, a character in one of Jean-Paul Sartre's plays says the following: "There was nothing left in heaven, no right or wrong, nor anyone to give me orders. . . . I . . . am a man, and every man must find out his own way."[2]

If nature were all there were to deal with, there would be no valid reason to resist natural tendencies and impulses; however, there is also vocation. In a certain sense, we could say the most "fulfilled" state of a human being is precisely to be "single for the sake of the kingdom," because people are "called" not to live in an eternal relationship as a couple but to live in eternal relationship with God.

There has been much discussion in the past about whether or not virginity and celibacy are a more perfect state than marriage and, if so, in what sense. I believe that celibacy is not *ontologically more perfect*: each of the two states of life is perfect for the person who is called to it. It is, however, a state in life that is *eschatologically more advanced*, in the sense that it more clearly approximates the definitive state toward which we are all journeying. St. Cyprian, a married man, wrote to the first Christian virgins, "What we shall be, already you have begun to be."[3]

MISSIONARY DIMENSION OF CELIBACY

This is the rationale for celibacy deriving from the fact that the kingdom of God has "already" come. In another sense, though, we said that the kingdom has "not yet" come but that it is still on its way. It must come in *intensity* within the Church and every believer, permeating the whole of life, and it must come in *extension* until it reaches the ends of the earth. The rationale for celibacy flows from that: Since the kingdom of God has not yet fully come but is still coming, there needs to be men and women who dedicate themselves full-time and wholeheartedly to the coming of this kingdom. This is the *missionary* or apostolic *dimension* of virginity and celibacy.

It is difficult to imagine what the face of the Catholic Church would look like today if there had not been a host of men and women throughout the ages who had renounced "home, spouse, and children" for the sake of the kingdom of heaven (see Lk 18:29). The proclamation of the gospel and the Church's mission have in large part rested on their shoulders. They have advanced our understanding of the Word of God through their studies; they have opened up new paths of Christian thought and spirituality; they have brought the proclamation of the kingdom to far-off nations; and they are the ones who brought into existence almost all the charitable institutions that have so enriched the Church and the world.

From what has been said so far, it becomes clear that celibacy signifies not sterility but, on the contrary, enormous fruitfulness. It is a different kind of fruitfulness, one that is spiritual and not physical. But since humankind is also a spirit and not just a body, it is a fruitfulness that is also exquisitely *human*. Christian people know very well that in every culture they have spontaneously called celibate men "Father" and virgins "Mother." How many priests are still simply called "Father" and how many sisters are still simply called "Mother" even after they have been proclaimed saints by the Church! We continue to speak of "Padre Pio of Pietrelcina" or of "Mother Teresa of Calcutta," as though the title of "Father" or "Mother" were more important than the title of "Saint" or "Blessed" with which the Church has invested them in the meantime.

It is this conviction that allows St. Paul to say, when addressing the Christians in Corinth, "For though you have countless guides in Christ, you do not have many fathers. For I became your father in Christ Jesus through the gospel" (1 Cor 4:15); it allows him to call the Galatians "My little children, with whom I am in travail until Christ be formed in you!" (Gal 4:19). So many affective crises in the lives of priests, with the disastrous consequences we are all aware of, are due to the absence of experiences of spiritual fatherhood, to an "impotence," so to speak, in generating children in the faith through the proclamation of the gospel. (I am glad to see there is a chapter in this book on the "fatherhood of the celibate priest.")

We hear a lot of talk these days about "the quality of life." People say that the most important thing is not to increase the amount of life on our planet but to raise its quality. However, there is also a *spiritual quality of life*, and that is even more important because it concerns people's souls, which are eternal. Those who are celibates and virgins for the sake of the kingdom are called to pour themselves out to raise this spiritual quality of life, not to mention they have also worked and are still working to raise the medical, social, and cultural quality of life. Recently a priest at the North American College in Rome, William J. Slattery, gave me a complimentary copy of one of his works in three volumes (not yet published) titled "Heroism and Genius: How Catholic Priests Built Western Civilization." It is perhaps not impartial historical research, but the facts he presents about the contribution of the Catholic priesthood (pope, bishops, and priests) in every field of knowledge and every aspect of civilization from their origins to the present are impressive.

At times, people criticize the Catholic Church for having given too broad an interpretation of Jesus' saying about being celibate for the kingdom by imposing it on all its priests. It seems far more serious that some Christian churches that claim to preach a "full gospel" lack any way of fulfilling this evangelical directive of celibacy for the sake of the kingdom. For more than ten years, I have been a member of the Catholic delegation to the ecumenical Dialogue with Pentecostals. Because of the peaceful and friendly atmosphere among us, I once allowed myself to joke in our meeting, "You always talk about the 'full gospel' that you preach," I said to them with a smile, "but it seems to me that your gospel is indeed full . . . but full of holes."

Since it is not of divine origin, the rule about mandatory celibacy for priests can of course be changed by the Church if at a certain point the Church thought it necessary. (I do not consider it within my purview to deal with this issue.) However, no one can honestly deny that, despite all the difficulties and defections, celibacy has enormously benefited the cause of the kingdom and of holiness and that it is still today a very efficacious sign of the kingdom in the midst of the Christian people.

SPOUSAL DIMENSION OF CELIBACY

Paul's text in 1 Corinthians 7 permits us to move now to another dimension of celibacy and virginity, the dimension I have called "spousal":

> The form of this world is passing away. I want you to be free from anxieties. The unmarried man is anxious about the affairs of the Lord, how to please the Lord; but the married man is anxious about worldly affairs, how to please his wife, and his interests are divided. And the unmarried woman or virgin is anxious about the affairs of the Lord, how to be holy in body and spirit; but the married woman is anxious about worldly affairs, how to please her husband. I say this for your benefit, not to lay any restraint upon you, but to promote good order and to secure your undivided devotion to the Lord. (1 Cor 7:31–35)

The apostle speaks about a divided heart and an undivided heart. Those who are married, he says, needing to be concerned with the affairs of the world and with pleasing a wife or a husband, find their interests "divided," while the voluntary renunciation of marriage allows a person to live with "undivided devotion to the Lord," that is, undivided within themselves and united to the Lord, which is the formula for authentic and perfect unity. As St. Augustine says, "By continence we are gathered together and brought back to the One, from whom we have dissipated our being with many things."[4]

Up to this point, it could be said that the motivation St. Paul gives for renouncing marriage is different than the one Jesus gives. It is a subjective—almost psychological—motive whose focus is the good of the individual, his or her inner peace and unity, more than for the sake of the kingdom of God. But that is not the case. All the reasons given by the apostle to choose virginity and celibacy are summarized in the phrase "for the Lord," and that phrase is the exact equivalent after Easter of the expression "for the kingdom of heaven."

However, a development occurs here concerning the meaning of celibacy and virginity that is owed not to St. Paul but to Jesus himself because, after dying and rising for us, he has become "the Lord" and has made the Church his spouse (see Eph 5:25). According to Matthew 19, one foregoes marrying "for the sake of the kingdom," that is, for a *cause*; according to the text of 1 Corinthians, one foregoes marriage "for the Lord," that is, for a *person*.

Let us examine a bit more closely what this implies. The apostle tells us he would like to see his faithful ones "without anxieties" (*amerimnous*). If one were to stop here, there is actually a danger of seeing celibacy as a wonderful opportunity to have a comfortable life without problems and anxieties. Who would not sign up for a life without anxieties? The Stoics and the Epicureans in Paul's day were following an ideal of this kind that they called apatheia or ataraxia, that is, living without emotional or passionate disturbances, ready to sacrifice everything, even joy and pleasures of the flesh that were too intense, to have that kind of inner peace.

But let us pay attention to what the apostle immediately adds. He says that the one who is "unmarried is anxious [*merimnà*] about the affairs of the Lord." This does not, therefore, point to an ideal of ataraxia, which means a life without worries. It is a life without worldly distractions so that one can have the time and availability to be concerned with the affairs of the Lord, that is, the souls for whom he died, the poor, in brief, the kingdom.

Also, it is not true that these people do not marry. We speak metaphorically about people who have "espoused" a cause when they have given themselves completely, body and soul, to a cause and made the interests, the risks, and the success of that cause their own. Don't we say that Karl Marx espoused the cause of the proletariat and Simone de Beauvoir that of feminism? How much more then do the celibate and the virgin claim to be married to the kingdom, having given themselves not just to a "cause" but also to a person.

Having risen from the dead, Jesus is alive and present in the world. He is the jealous spouse who reproves the Church at Ephesus of having abandoned their "first love" (see Rv 2:4). It is not a question then of the celibate or the virgin renouncing a "concrete" love for an "abstract" love, that is, of renouncing a real person for an imaginary one. It is a question of renouncing a concrete love for another concrete love, of renouncing a real person for a person who is infinitely more real.

Rabbi Simeon ben Azzai, a Jewish rabbi in the same century as St. Paul, a keen scholar of the Mosaic law, challenging the common mind-set of his fellow countrymen, refused to marry and offered the following justification that one reads in the Talmud: "My soul clings lovingly to the Torah; let others contribute to the preservation of the race."[5] With even more reason, the Christian celibate and virgin can make these words their own and say, "My soul is in love with Jesus Christ. Let others contribute to the preservation of human race."

Love suffers at times from an unfortunate bifurcation, which the theologian Anders Nygren sought to justify theologically in his famous work titled *Agape and Eros*.[6] On the one hand, there is agape, divine love that comes down, which is pure gift, compassion, and grace. On the other hand, there is human love, eros, which instead involves a search, desire, and a presumption of saving oneself through one's own efforts, giving something back to God in exchange. The relationship between agape and eros, according to Nygren, is modeled on the relationship that Luther sees between faith and works. There is no place for eros in our relationship with God, as the New Testament demonstrates by excluding this word from its vocabulary.[7]

The result of this process is the radical secularization of eros, which is now made completely worldly. While a certain dialectical theology was excluding eros from agape, secular culture, for its part, was only too happy to perform the opposite process of excluding agape from eros and thus removing every reference to God and to grace from human love. Sigmund Freud followed this line of thinking to its extreme, reducing love to eros and eros to libido, to mere sexual instinct.

Pope Benedict XVI in his encyclical *Deus caritas est* rightly rejected this opposition and spoke of eros and agape as two dimensions or movements of love that are both present whether in God's love for human beings or in human beings' love for God and for one another.

> *Eros* and *agape*—ascending love and descending love— can never be completely separated. . . . Biblical faith does not set up a parallel universe, or one opposed to that primordial human phenomenon which is love, but rather accepts the whole man; it intervenes in his search for love in order to purify it and to reveal new dimensions of it.[8]

This reconciliation of the two loves has implications not only for spousal love but also for the love of celibates and virgins. Somewhere I read the following description of the two musical genres "hot jazz" and "cool jazz," although I know there are other ways of characterizing them. "Hot jazz" is passionate, fiery, expressive, arising from outbursts of feelings and leading to original improvisations. "Cool jazz" occurs when the music turns professional: the emotions become repetitious; technique is substituted for inspiration; virtuosity is substituted for spontaneity; and the musician plays more from the head than from the heart.

Often the love in which celibates are formed has something of "cool jazz" about it. It is a love that comes "from the head" and more through the exercise of the will than from any intimate movement in the heart. It is shaped in a preset mold, rather than each person giving expression to his or her own unique and unrepeatable love that corresponds to the uniqueness of each person before God. Acts of love toward God in this case are like those of inexperienced lovers who write their beloved a love letter that has been copied out of a book.

If worldly love is a body without a soul, this kind of religious love is a soul without a body. A human being is not an angel, that is, a pure spirit. Rather, a human being is a body and soul that are substantially united. Everything a human being does, including love, necessarily reflects this structure. If the human component linked to affection and to the heart is systematically denied or repressed, there are two results: people either wearily drag themselves forward out of a sense of duty or to protect their image or find compensations that range from what is more or less licit to those very sad cases we know so well.

The strength and beauty of priestly celibacy consists in a love for Christ that is comprised of agape and eros, that is, of sacrifice, of the gift of oneself, and of faithfulness, but also of desire, joy, passion, and admiration. Nicholas Cabasilas writes, "From the beginning human desire was made to be gauged and measured by desire for Him, and is a treasury so great, so ample, that it is able to encompass even God. . . . He, then, is the [soul's] repose because He alone is goodness and truth and anything else it desires."[9]

Is it possible, people ask us, to fall in love in this life with someone who cannot be seen or touched? This is the crucial point. The resurrection allows us to think about Christ not as someone in the past but as a person who is alive and present with whom we can speak, whom we can also "touch" since, as Augustine says, "Whoever believes in Christ touches Christ."[10]

Jesus is the perfect man; in him are found, to an infinitely superior degree, all those qualities and expressions of personal attention that a man looks for in a woman and a woman looks for in a man. His love does not necessarily insulate us from the appeal of other beings and in particular the attraction of the opposite sex. This is part of our nature that God himself created and does not want to destroy. His love gives us, however, the strength to overcome these other attractions because of an attraction that is more powerful. "A chaste man," writes John Climacus, "is someone who has driven out eros by means of eros,"[11] meaning in the first case carnal love and in the second case love for Christ. Celibacy without an ardent love of Christ—or at least a strong desire for that love—is an empty shell, comparable to a marriage without love.

CHARISMATIC DIMENSION OF CELIBACY

We come now to the last dimension of celibacy I intend to discuss, the pneumatic or charismatic dimension. Let us begin with the passage from Paul in 1 Corinthians 7:25: "Now concerning the unmarried I have no command of the Lord, but I give my *opinion*" (*gnome*, translated in the Vulgate as *consilium*). In the past, perfect chastity—as well as voluntary poverty and obedience—was explained mostly in the category of "evangelical counsels." A clear summary of this doctrine, to which we always return, is that of St. Thomas Aquinas in his *Summa Theologica*.[12]

The limitation of the concept of "counsel" is that it belongs more to the realm of law than of grace, more to duty than to gift. It is worthwhile, therefore, for us to see what can be newly understood if we make use of a different category, the one that the apostle himself uses in this same context: the category of charism. "Each," he says, "has his own special gift [charisma] from God, one of one kind and one of another" (1 Cor 7:7), that is, the married person has his or her charism and the virgin has his or her charism.

St. Cyril of Jerusalem, along with many others, considered "the strength to remain chaste" among the number of charisms given by the Spirit, alongside poverty and martyrdom.[13] The idea of "gift" is implied in the very words with which Jesus instituted celibacy for the sake of the kingdom when he said that not everyone could receive this, saying "but only those to whom it is given [*dedotai*]" to understand (see Mt 19:11).

If celibacy or virginity is essentially a charism, then it is a "manifestation of the Spirit," because that is how a charism is defined in the New Testament (see 1 Cor 12:7). If it is a charism, then it is more a gift *received* from God than a gift *given* to God. A charism is a *gratia gratis data*, a free gift. The saying of Jesus that "you did not choose me, but I chose you" (Jn 15:16) applies, then, to celibates and virgins in a special way. One chooses celibacy not to enter into the kingdom but because the kingdom has entered into one. You do not remain celibate to better save your soul but because the Lord has taken hold of you, has chosen you, and you feel the need to remain free to respond fully to this calling.

What stands out here is the need for a conversion that consists in moving from an attitude of individuals believing they have offered a gift and made a sacrifice to the completely different attitude of individuals realizing they have received a gift and must first of all express thanks. I believe there is not one consecrated person who has not understood or intuited at some time, especially at the blossoming of the vocation, that what they were receiving was the greatest grace from God for them after baptism.

The Marks of True Celibacy: Humility, Freedom, and Joy

If celibacy is a charism, then it must be lived charismatically, that is, the way a person usually relates to a gift—above all with *humility*. "What have you that you did not receive? If then you received it, why do you boast as if it were not a gift?" (1 Cor 4:7). The martyr Ignatius of Antioch wrote, "If anyone is able to persevere in chastity to the honor of the flesh of the Lord, let him do so in all humility. If he is boastful about it, he is lost."[14] Some fathers, like St. Jerome, St. Augustine, and St. Bernard, ended up even saying that "an incontinent person who is humble is better than a proud celibate."

Celibates are more exposed than other people to the temptation of pride and self-sufficiency. They have never knelt before a creature acknowledging their incompleteness and their need for the other; they have never, like a beggar, stretched out their hand to another human being, saying, "Give yourself to me because I, by myself, am not complete," which is what a young man says when he declares his love to a young woman.

To live chastity with humility means not presuming on one's own strength, recognizing one's vulnerability, and leaning only on God's grace through prayer. St. Augustine said,

> I believed that continence lay within a man's own powers, and such powers I was not conscious of within myself. I was so foolish that I did not know that, as it is written, no man can be continent unless you grant it to him [see Wisdom 8:21]. This you would surely have given, if with inward groanings I had knocked at your ears and with a firm faith had cast all my cares upon you.[15]

We know Augustine's cry of victory once he discovered this truth: "Oh, God, you command me to be continent; well, give me what you command and then command me as you will."[16]

Secondly, if celibacy is a gift of the Spirit, it must be lived with *freedom* because "where the Spirit of the Lord is, there is freedom" (2 Cor 3:17). This liberty is of course internal, not external, and signifies the absence of psychological problems, scruples, uneasiness, and fear. A great wrong was done to celibacy and virginity in the past when that state of life was enveloped by a swarm of fears, misgivings, and admonitions to "be careful about this, and be careful about that!" making this vocation the kind of path where all the signposts read, "Danger! Danger!" It ended up moving sexuality into a completely profane context in which God is in the way and must be excluded. It has become a topic that is spoken about through subtexts with double meanings and always with some malice and guilt. This is an enormous wrong against God. It is as if the devil, and not God, were the specialist in love! We need to stand against this usurpation.

In order to live the charism of celibacy with freedom, it is helpful to have a healthy consciousness and acceptance of the sexual dimension of our lives. Human sexuality, as we know today, is not confined solely to its procreative function but has a vast range of possibilities and resonances within a person, some of which are fully valid for celibates and virgins. The celibate and the virgin have renounced the active exercise of sexuality but not sexuality itself. It is not something we leave behind. It remains and "informs" so many expressions of a person. The celibate does not cease being a man, nor does the virgin cease being a woman.

This fact is also recognized by psychology, which acknowledges the possibility of "sublimating" sexual instinct without destroying it, of spiritualizing it and making it serve goals that are equally worthy of human beings. The sublimation process can be ambiguous if it is unconscious and directed toward creating surrogates, but it can also be positive and indicative of maturity if it is supported by sound motives and lived in freedom. There are celibates not only for the sake of the kingdom; there have been celibates for the sake of art, for scholarship, and for other noble goals in life.

A healthy understanding of sex also helps a person to have a calm, clear picture—insofar as possible given our present condition compromised by sin—of the whole of created reality, including the transmission of life. We need to look at the opposite sex, falling in love, and procreation with clear eyes. We need, in short, to have eyes like Jesus. What liberty he had in speaking about all these things and in using them as metaphors and parables for spiritual realities!

We should not be surprised or unduly worried if at certain times we experience the strong "appeal" of the opposite sex and, for us priests, an attraction to women. That is not wrong; it is simply natural. It goes back to the fact that, "in the beginning, God created them male and female" (see Gn 1:27). We should not hide behind a screen of false angelicalness or defend ourselves by using coarse language to show off our freedom to the opposite sex, which is precisely what is lacking. Instead, we need to make use of that "appeal" and attraction to the opposite sex and offer it as a special part of our "living sacrifice." We need to say to ourselves, "Well, this is exactly what I have chosen to offer up for the kingdom and for the Lord."

Finally, if chastity for the sake of the kingdom is a charism, it should be lived with *joy*. In the past, priests and religious, through the color of their habits and other signs, have chosen to testify primarily to their renunciation of the world. It would be just as appropriate to testify to the other aspect of their charism: the anticipation in faith and hope of the splendor and the joy of the heavenly Jerusalem when the bride will "be clothed with fine linen, bright and pure" (Rv 19:8). This means, in brief, remembering not only the moment of the cross in the paschal mystery but also the moment of the resurrection.

The best advertisement for vocations is a joyful, calm, peaceful priest. Through his simple life, he testifies that Jesus is capable of filling his life and making him happy. I have sometimes had the impression when participating in events promoting vocations that the invitation to a priestly vocation and to religious life has been made with the following unspoken but clear subtext: "embrace our life, even though it entails celibacy; you will be able to contribute to the coming of the kingdom, help the poor, raise people's consciousness, live free from slavery to things, and promote social justice." I believe we should simply repent of having such little faith and have the courage to invite young men to embrace the vocation of priesthood not *in spite of* celibacy but *because* of it, or at least *also* because of it.

Celibacy and Marriage

One of the most important consequences of speaking about virginity and celibacy in terms of being charisms is the decisive elimination of the latent opposition between chastity for the kingdom and marriage, an opposition that has plagued both these Christian vocations. I love the Fathers of the Church very much, but on this point I am constrained, just this once, to express certain reservations in their regard. The treatises *On Virginity*, both by the Greek Fathers and the Latin Fathers, dedicate about half their pages to highlighting the evils of marriage without ever reaching the point of discussing marriage itself, just as the Manicheans did.[17]

In the New Testament, as we have seen, celibacy and virginity have an essentially positive rational: the kingdom and the Lord. With the Fathers, little by little this state of life acquires a primarily negative and ascetic rationale, which is the renunciation of marriage and the bridling of one's passions. In the New Testament the motive ("for the kingdom" and "for the Lord") takes precedence over the decision to not marry; with the Fathers the renunciation of marriage tends to take precedence over the motive for celibacy, even if that motive is still clearly present.

If we begin with the vantage point of charism and vocation, these two states of life can finally be fully reconciled and even build each other up. A charism, St. Paul says, "is a manifestation of the Spirit *for the common good*" (1 Cor 12:7). St. Peter affirms the same thing when he writes, "As each has received a gift [charisma], employ it for one another" (1 Pt 4:10). Applied to our case, this means that celibacy is also for the sake of married people; it is not a private affair or a personal choice for one's path to perfection. It is "for the common good" and "for the service of one another." The same is true for marriage.

Married people are reminded of the primacy of God and of that which does not pass away by those who are consecrated. They are introduced to a love for the Word of God, which those who are consecrated—and have more time and availability— are able to study more in depth and to "break open" for their brothers and sisters. But celibates also have much to learn from married people. They learn generosity, self-forgetfulness, service to others, and often a certain human quality that comes from direct contact with the tragedies of life.

In many religious orders, including mine, there was a rule in force until a few decades ago about getting up at night to recite the office of Matins. Then things changed. It seemed that the rhythm of modern life, the young men's studies, and the apostolic ministry of the older men no longer allowed for this nightly rising. Little by little that custom was abandoned in the vast majority of cases. Once I became a priest, however, the Lord brought me to various families through my ministry and, in particular, a group of young couples with small children. I then discovered something that startled me, but in a good way: those fathers and mothers had to get up not once but three or four times a night to feed or administer medicine or rock the baby if it cried or keep watch over it if it had a fever. And in the morning one of the two parents, or both, had to rush off to work after taking the baby to the grandparents or to day care because there was a timecard to punch, and they had to do so regardless of the weather and regardless of their own good or bad health.

I then said to myself, if our way of life is not supported by pastoral zeal and a certain rigor in our schedule and habits, it is in danger of becoming a comfortable life that could lead to hardness of heart. What good parents are capable of doing for their biological children—the level of self-forgetfulness that they are capable of attaining to provide for their children's well-being, their studies, and their happiness—must be the measure of what we should do for our spiritual children and for the poor. This is the example set by the apostle Paul himself when he said to his spiritual children in Corinth, "I will most gladly spend and be spent for your souls" (2 Cor 12:15).

An accurate understanding of married people's lives helps us not to have a false idea of marriage, which is what films and television shows portray. It teaches us a healthy realism that is so necessary for anyone who proclaims the Word of God. It makes us discover the benefits, and not just the sacrifices, of celibacy, and it makes us alert to and cognizant of the problems and difficulties married people have. Those who are urging the abolition of mandatory celibacy for priests should beware, in my opinion, of the illusion that all the problems of the clergy would be resolved by its abolition.

I conclude with an elegy of Catholic priesthood and celibacy written by the famous French Dominican Henri-Dominique Lacordaire. Particularly in these times, this could seem idealistic and unrealistic, but instead it is completely true and deserved by so many priests. It is good for everyone to hear it again, at least as an ideal to pursue and as something to point out to young men who will come after us.

> To live in the midst of the world, with no desire for its pleasures; to be a member of every family, yet belonging to none; to share all sufferings, to penetrate all secrets, to heal all wounds; to go daily from men to God, to offer Him their homage and petitions, to return from God to men, to bring them His pardon and His hope; to have a heart of iron for chastity and a heart of flesh for charity; to teach and to pardon, console and bless, and to be blessed forever. O God, what a life is this, and it is thine, O priest of Jesus Christ.[18]

2

Friends of the Bridegroom: The Biblical Foundations of Priestly Celibacy

Mary Healy, STD

I s the discipline of priestly celibacy of biblical origin, or did it arise only in Church tradition of the patristic era with its ascetic ideals? If it is of biblical origin, what is its deepest rationale? These questions of immense theological and pastoral importance illustrate in a particularly striking way the interdependence of sacred scripture and sacred tradition. The New Testament teaching on celibacy arose out of the living tradition of the early Church, which was itself rooted in the traditions of Israel. The scriptures are in turn normative for subsequent tradition, yet our understanding of what the scriptures say is deeply conditioned by how the Church has received, interpreted, and lived these texts in its tradition. In the case of priestly celibacy, the question is complicated by the fact that two very different lines of interpretation have developed in the Christian East and

West. Further, in the West the main lines of reasoning for the discipline have changed over time, as the emphasis has shifted from priestly *continence* within marriage (in the early centuries when many clerics were married) to priestly *celibacy*.[1]

Most of the recent studies of the origins of clerical celibacy focus on patristic writings and on ecclesiastical legislation from the fourth century on, with only brief discussion of the biblical material.[2] This lack of attention is not surprising, considering that the relevant biblical texts are few and tend to be oblique and suggestive rather than direct. In this chapter I will explore these biblical foundations by examining first the Old Testament background and then the teaching of the gospels and of Paul on celibacy. I will consider whether the New Testament indicates any intrinsic relationship between celibacy and the priesthood and what the underlying logic would be of such a relationship. Finally, I'll examine two passages that seem to present counterevidence to a biblical basis for clerical celibacy and offer an alternative way of interpreting these texts.

Celibacy in the Old Testament

To appreciate the New Testament's teaching on celibacy it is crucial first to recognize that in ancient Israel celibacy as a religious ideal simply did not exist. In Israelite tradition there is no greater human blessing than that of marriage and children. It is the primordial blessing given to humanity at the moment of creation: "God blessed them and said to them, be fruitful and multiply" (Gn 1:28). It is likewise the foundational blessing bestowed on Abraham at the origin of the chosen people: "I will make you exceedingly fruitful; I will make nations of you, and kings shall come forth from you" (Gn 17:6).[3] Marriage is thus *"a religiously privileged state*, privileged by revelation itself."[4] Conversely, to be deprived of the gift of marriage and children was considered the greatest of misfortunes. The esteem in which Israel held marriage is poignantly illustrated in the story of Jephthah's daughter, who was doomed to be offered in sacrifice because of her father's rash vow. She begs his permission to first go into the mountains for two months to "mourn her virginity"

(Jgs 11:37–38)—that is, to mourn the fact that she dies a virgin. In the context of the old covenant, to freely choose celibacy and childlessness as a state of life was simply unthinkable. Priestly celibacy would of course have been nonsensical, since the primary qualification for priesthood was physical descent from the family of Aaron.

Only one instance of voluntary celibacy is recorded in the Old Testament: that of the prophet Jeremiah. But his celibacy had a meaning and motivation entirely different from later Christian practice. God required the prophet to forego marriage, not as a positive commitment to God but as a prophetic sign of imminent disaster (Jer 16:1–4). In typical prophetic style, Jeremiah personally embodied his message. His celibacy was a graphic symbol of the terrifying judgment to come upon apostate Judah, in which women and children would perish by disease, sword, and famine without lament or burial.[5]

The Old Testament's negative view of the unmarried state is widely reflected in later rabbinic writings. According to rabbinic tradition, "Be fruitful and multiply" (Gn 1:28) is the first of the 613 commandments that Jewish men are required to observe.[6] For a man to remain unmarried past the age of twenty was considered blameworthy.[7] The Talmud records the well-known saying of Rabbi Eleazar: "Any man who has no wife is no man."[8] Despite this general disapproval, however, in the intertestamental period there were some instances of celibacy as a freely chosen lifestyle. Some members of the Essene community practiced celibacy, although the evidence is inconclusive as to whether it was obligatory or merely encouraged. Clearly, it was linked with ritual purity and with a highly negative view of women.[9] Philo also mentions the example of the Therapeutae, a Jewish sect in Egypt.[10] The closest parallel to Christian celibacy is the intriguing example of the late first-century Rabbi Simeon ben Azzai, who paradoxically disapproved of celibacy yet practiced it himself. When challenged by his fellow rabbis, he replied, "But what shall I do, seeing that my soul is in love with the Torah? The world can be carried on by others."[11] All these instances, however, were exceptions to the Jewish norm, in which the failure to take a wife and bear offspring was frowned on as a transgression of a divine command.

With respect to *temporary* sexual abstinence, however, we find an entirely different situation. At several points the Old Testament bears witness to a close relationship between sexual abstinence and contact with the holy. This link first appears in the Exodus account of the theophany on Mount Sinai, the event that gave birth to Israel as a nation. Here God establishes a priestly status for all Israel: "You shall be to me a kingdom of priests and a holy nation" (Ex 19:6). He then commands that in preparation for the theophany on the third day the people "consecrate themselves" and "wash their garments" (19:10)—actions closely linked with priesthood (cf. Ex 40:13; Nm 19:7). To these injunctions Moses adds, "Be ready by the third day; do not go near a woman" (19:15), that is, abstain from marital relations. Although the reasoning is left implicit, the notion that a direct encounter with God requires abstinence may reflect the idea that sexual intercourse causes a certain preoccupation with what is earthly, a diverting of energies that precludes fixing one's undivided attention and ardor on the holy God. It is significant that in the Pentateuchal narrative this stipulation is given *prior* to the ritual purity laws of Leviticus. At this point in Exodus there is no suggestion of sexual relations causing impurity; it is a matter of passing not from the unclean to the clean but from the profane (common) realm to the holy. Only *after* the watershed event of the golden calf idolatry with its (probably cultic) sexual revelry (cf. Ex 32:6, 25)—a particularly egregious abuse of the sexual faculty—is the ritual purity legislation instituted specifying that intercourse renders one unclean. This suggests that the abstinence rule expressed here embodies an enduring principle that does not belong to those ritual purity laws abrogated in the new covenant.[12]

Interestingly, later rabbinic commentary, despite its negative view of celibacy, held that, from the Sinai theophany on, Moses remained permanently continent. His abiding proximity to God (in contrast to Israel's temporary proximity) was viewed as requiring the permanent renunciation of sexual relations. According to the Talmud, Moses reasoned to himself,

> If the Israelites, with whom the *Shekhinah* [the divine presence] spoke only on one occasion and He appointed them a [definite] time, yet the Torah said, "Be ready for the third day: do not come near a woman": I, with whom the *Shekhinah* speaks at all times and does not appoint me a [definite] time, how much more so![13]

The link between sexual abstinence and proximity to God is codified in Leviticus, though now with an explicit reference to ritual purity.[14] Since sexual intercourse rendered a person temporarily unclean (Lv 15:18, 32; cf. Dt 23:10–14), priests were required to observe abstinence during their terms of temple service—a requirement mentioned explicitly in regard to the eating of sacrificed food (Lv 22:4–7). Abstinence was also required of soldiers on active duty, engaged in the sacred duty of fighting the Lord's battles (cf. 1 Sm 21:4–5).[15]

Although this Old Testament background is rarely invoked today in discussions of the theology of celibacy, it is the essential backdrop to New Testament teaching for two reasons. First, scripture's unambiguous affirmation of the good of marriage helps ensure that Christian celibacy is not founded on a denigration of the married state or on a view of sexuality as intrinsically tainted—a mistake too often made in early Christianity. Second, the Old Testament regulations on temporary sexual abstinence provide an important though subtle clue to the link between celibacy and ordained ministry in the New Testament.

CELIBACY IN THE TEACHING OF JESUS

At the dawn of the new covenant, in the angel Gabriel's dialogue with Mary, is the announcement of something entirely new: a fruitful virginity. Gabriel assures Mary that, although she does "not know man" (Lk 1:34), by the power of the Holy Spirit she will bring forth a child who is the Son of God—a fruitfulness that infinitely surpasses anything envisioned in the old covenant. Since Luke portrays Mary as an icon of the Christian community,[16] Mary's virginity is the first hint of a new, supernatural kind of espousal and fruitfulness for the Church, although during Jesus' earthly life this mystery remained hidden from his contemporaries. Luke's account of the annunciation and visitation also portrays Mary as the new ark of the covenant—the true dwelling place of the living God, of which the original ark was only a foreshadowing.[17] Joseph, then, is in the role of priest, chastely ministering to God's hidden presence in the humble home at Nazareth.

The only direct reference to celibacy in Jesus' public ministry is a remarkably brief saying recorded in Matthew—significantly, in the context of an affirmation of marriage. When Jesus declares that marriage is indissoluble, the disciples protest, "If that is the case of a man with his wife, it is better not to marry" (Mt 19:10). This complaint becomes the occasion for a new pronouncement on the voluntary renunciation of marriage (for an entirely different reason than the defeatist pragmatism of the disciples):

> Not everyone can receive this saying, but only those to whom it is given. There are eunuchs who have been so from birth, and there are eunuchs who have been made eunuchs by men, and there are eunuchs who have made themselves eunuchs for the sake of the kingdom of heaven. He who is able to receive this, let him receive it. (Mt 19:11–12)

This saying, which may sound harsh to us, would have been even more so in the cultural context of the day. The term "eunuch" had highly pejorative, even offensive, connotations.[18] As a man with a physical defect, a eunuch was ineligible for priesthood and barred from any participation in the temple worship of God's people (Lv 21:20–21; Dt 23:1).[19] It is even possible that "eunuch" was a term of opprobrium that Jesus' opponents had thrown at him because of his unmarried state, which he picked up and used for his own purposes, as he did with other epithets such as glutton, drunkard, blasphemer, friend of tax collectors, and sinners.[20]

Jesus' saying is framed by a double affirmation that what he proposes applies not to all his followers but only to some: "Those to whom it is given" (Mt 19:11a) or one "who is able to receive this" (v. 12b). That is, celibacy for the kingdom is a charism, a gift freely given by God to whomever he wills, which must in turn be freely accepted by the individual. In a characteristically Semitic way, Jesus sets the context for his saying by noting the obvious fact of life that some men are eunuchs by genetic defect and some by castration. This negative context serves to underscore the daring newness of his pronouncement: "There are eunuchs who have made themselves eunuchs for the sake of the kingdom of heaven."[21] As Pope John Paul II points out in his theology of the body catecheses, in the context of salvation history Jesus' saying is an "absolute novelty," a "turning point" in the revelation of the meaning of the body.[22]

By using the severe term "eunuch" as a metaphor for voluntary celibacy, Jesus alludes to the self-denial entailed in such a call, that it involves the renunciation of the primordial blessing and the ordinary path to happiness in human life. Yet, he asserts, there is a supreme value, a supernatural good, that relativizes all natural goods and thus motivates such renunciation, namely, "the kingdom of heaven." The kingdom of heaven—Matthew's circumlocution for "the kingdom of God," an expression that sums up Israel's hopes for the manifest reign of God over his people and all creation[23]—is the central object of all Jesus' preaching and public ministry. The kingdom is already present in Jesus himself and the community formed around him yet mysteriously hidden and to come in its fullness only at the end of time. That some would renounce marriage "for the sake of the kingdom" is a prophetic testimony to the reality of the kingdom, already present here and now.[24] Even more, it is an eschatological sign pointing to the full consummation of the kingdom. In his later dialogue with the Sadducees, Jesus declares that "in the resurrection they neither marry nor are given in marriage, but are like angels in heaven" (Mt 22:30). Those who are celibate for the kingdom, then, anticipate in a visible way this final destiny of human life. They "step beyond the dimensions of history—while still living within the dimensions of history—and dramatically declare to the world that *the kingdom of God is here* (Mt 12:28)."[25]

In his profound reflection on these texts, John Paul II writes that Jesus' words imply that, in the resurrected life, the spousal meaning of the body—that is, its sexual complementarity designed for spousal union—will be revealed "as the *'virginal'* meaning of being male and female."[26] Marriage will come to an end only because it will give way to that which it is designed to prefigure: the heavenly wedding—an immeasurably greater exchange of love in which each person will "express all the energies of his own personal and . . . psychosomatic subjectivity."[27] Each person's gift of self to God will be his or her eternal response to the living experience of *"God's most personal 'self-giving': in his very divinity to man."*[28] The risen human body will become the vehicle and expression of a reciprocal self-donation to God, and to all the redeemed, that will be virginal yet will infinitely transcend the earthly one-flesh union of husband and wife. Celibates, by witnessing to the fulfillment found in self-donation apart from sexual intimacy, are signs of the joy of the future kingdom already anticipated here on earth.

But there is a further significance to Jesus' saying on eunuchs. The fact that he is offering not only an invitation for his disciples but also the explanation of his own virginity implies that celibacy for the kingdom is ultimately rooted in the mystery of Christ himself. It takes on its full significance only in relation to him. Why was Jesus celibate? This question must be answered in light of his affirmation of his identity elsewhere in the Gospel. In Matthew 9:15, in response to a question about why his disciples do not fast, Jesus replies, "Can the wedding guests mourn as long as the bridegroom is with them? The days will come, when the bridegroom is taken away from them, and then they will fast." With this saying he alludes to the Old Testament theme of the spousal covenant between Yʜwʜ and Israel,[29] and in a veiled way identifies *himself* as the God who desires to wed his people. As John Paul II notes, the nuptial theme is not just one among many strands of imagery in scripture; rather, it is the Bible's deepest symbolic key for expressing the relationship between God and man. "As God's salvific plan for humanity, that [spousal] mystery is in some sense the central theme of the whole of revelation, its central reality."[30] The spousal theme runs through the whole of biblical revelation, from the nuptial scene in the garden at the dawn of creation (Gn 2:21–25), through the Song of Songs, which both Jewish and Christian tradition consider a mystical allegory of the romance between God and his people, and to the "marriage of the Lamb" at the end (Rv 19:7; 21:9).

Jesus further discloses this mystery through the parables of the ten virgins and of the king who gives a wedding banquet for his son (Mt 22:1–14; 25:1–13), which portray his coming as the joyous announcement of the Messianic nuptials so long promised by the prophets. The same imagery is at work in the story of the wedding at Cana (Jn 2:1–11). By providing a superabundance of new wine,[31] Jesus manifests himself as the Messianic bridegroom who has come to fulfill God's promises and establish a new, everlasting covenant of marriage with his people. Mary appears as the symbol and personification of the bride. Her response, "Do whatever he tells you" (Jn 2:5), echoes the acclamation of the people at Sinai, exemplifying the perfect response to God's covenant love (cf. Ex 19:8; 24:3, 7).[32] The entire Cana event, which takes place "on the third day" (Jn 2:1), is structured as a symbolic foreshadowing of Christ's passion, the definitive consummation of the nuptial covenant.[33] Jesus was celibate, then, precisely *because he is the divine bridegroom*, the Incarnate Son who embodies God's ineffable, undivided, faithful, and eternal love for his people. His identity and mission would be completely incompatible with marriage to a human individual. Far from being a refusal to marry, his celibacy is intrinsically nuptial.

This spousal character of Jesus' celibacy is concretely manifested in his public ministry. His unmarried state, far from distancing him from human relationships, enabled him to draw close to every person.[34] Precisely because he had no human family, he was free to be available to all and to belong to all—to enjoy their company at table, to heal their diseases, to welcome and show affection to children, and to reveal the Father's unfathomable love for each person he encountered. As bridegroom, Jesus also becomes the founder of the new Messianic family: "Whoever does the will of my Father in heaven is my brother, and sister, and mother" (Mt 12:50; cf. Jn 19:26).

Jesus' identity as bridegroom is, then, the deepest rationale of celibacy for the kingdom. This means that, for his disciples, the celibate vocation cannot be grounded in a primarily practical motive—a calculation of advantages in time, energy, and availability for mission.[35] Those who are drawn to accept Jesus' call are drawn primarily not to his cause but to *him*. Their hearts are captivated by the divine bridegroom such that their whole identity is founded in him (cf. Phil 3:12). Having experienced the presence of the kingdom in him, they desire to devote themselves wholly to him, to embody and share in a particular way his spousal self-donation to God's people.[36]

The Gospel of John expresses this desire with particular clarity in the words of John the Baptist, who almost certainly was celibate himself and thus anticipated the celibacy for the kingdom: "He who has the bride is the bridegroom; the friend of the bridegroom, who stands and hears him, rejoices greatly at the bridegroom's voice; therefore this joy of mine is now full. He must increase, but I must decrease" (Jn 3:29–30). Significantly, John, the archetype of the celibate ascetic, sacrificed his life to defend the sanctity of marriage (Mt 14:3–11). John's celibate life, devoted to announcing the bridegroom Messiah, is a prototype of Christian celibacy. There is only one bridegroom, but those who are celibate for the kingdom are friends of the bridegroom, who help prepare the Messianic wedding.[37] Like John, they draw attention not to themselves but to him (cf. 2 Cor 4:5). By the witness of their lives they cry out, "Behold, the bridegroom! Come out to meet him" (Mt 25:6; cf. Rv 22:17). It is not coincidental that the other well-known celibate of the New Testament, Paul, describes his ministry in a similar way, writing to the Corinthians, "I feel a divine jealousy for you, for I betrothed you to Christ to present you as a pure bride to her one husband" (2

Cor 11:2). Paul too is a friend of bridegroom, whose apostolic vocation entails both imaging Christ's "jealous" spousal love and helping the Church-bride to fully reciprocate that love.

CELIBACY IN THE TEACHING OF PAUL

Paul's instructions concerning marriage and celibacy in 1 Corinthians 7 could be considered a practical application of the teaching and example of Christ, based on his own pastoral experience in the early churches.[38] Paul, like Jesus, makes clear that, although he recommends celibacy, both marriage and celibacy are charisms, that is, gifts of grace that spring entirely from God's initiative and the individual's free acceptance. "I wish that all were as I myself am [i.e., celibate]. But each has his own charism [charisma] from God, one of one kind and one of another" (1 Cor 7:7). It would be a drastic misinterpretation to hold that Paul's advice stems from a denigration of marriage. In fact, his affirmation of the charism of celibacy *elevates* marriage by guaranteeing that marriage too is a freely embraced vocation and not a default position. For Paul, charisms are distinct from natural gifts or aptitudes in that they are permanently dependent on the working of the Holy Spirit. To live the charism of either marriage or celibacy requires an unceasing reliance on the Spirit's power.

Paul bases his exhortation to celibacy on a twofold motive that parallels the teaching of Christ.[39] First there is an eschatological motive. Because "the form of this world is passing away" (1 Cor 7:31), even those who have wives should "live as though they had none" (1 Cor 7:29). As good and holy as marriage is, it is relativized by the supreme value of the kingdom (cf. Lk 14:26). Celibates, because they are free of the this-worldly cares and anxieties attendant on married life, are able to fix their gaze on the world that is to come. Their lives are a prophetic sign to their fellow Christians that "our commonwealth is in heaven, and from it we await a Savior" (Phil 3:20). The celibate vocation is, then, the visible symbol of Christ's lordship over time. In the [celibate or] consecrated virgin the Church proclaims that time is . . . bathed already in the glory of the resurrection and the dawn of the parousia. The [celibate or] virgin is the witness to this divine fact, much like the snowcapped peak that catches the first light of the sunrise and heralds the day to a sleeping world.[40]

At the same time, the fact that even married Christians are called to live as if they were unmarried (1 Cor 7:29) suggests that Paul does not view celibacy as radically distinguishing one class from others within the Church. Rather, the advent of the kingdom leads all Christians to practice sexual self-restraint in one mode or another.[41] The dominance of the sex drive has been deposed in the face of an immeasurably greater love "hidden beneath the surface of all smaller loves."[42]

Second, the celibate vocation has an apostolic dimension, allowing people freedom to devote themselves entirely to the spread of the kingdom. "The unmarried man is anxious about the affairs of the Lord, how to please the Lord; but the married man is anxious about worldly affairs, how to please his wife, and his interests are divided" (1 Cor 7:32–34). As with Christ's teaching, it would be a mistake to interpret this in a utilitarian manner.[43] The motive of this commitment is primarily the desire "to please the Lord"—that is, to live a deep friendship with Christ the bridegroom Messiah[44]—and only secondarily the greater freedom and flexibility for his service.

CELIBACY AND THE PRIESTHOOD

But what does the institution of celibacy have to do with the priesthood? Is Jesus' saying simply a general invitation to his followers, or is it in any way intrinsically linked with apostleship and thus with ordained ministry in the church?

It is noteworthy that Jesus' institution of celibacy for the kingdom takes place in the context of his itinerant preaching, a missionary lifestyle of poverty, and total dependence on God. The apostles are called to share in this lifestyle, giving up the comforts of home and family to devote themselves full-time to the spread of the kingdom (cf. Mt 10:5–25). Peter implicitly seeks acknowledgment of this sacrifice when he says, "See, we have left our homes and followed you." Jesus' response, in Luke's version, includes "wife" in those things that are given up: "Truly, I say to you, there is no one who has left house or wife or brothers or parents or children, for the sake of the kingdom of God, who will not receive manifold more in this time, and in the age to come eternal life" (Lk 18:28–30; cf. 14:26).[45] What this meant in the case of Peter, who was or had been married (cf. Lk 4:38), is not specified. But clearly, the giving up of a wife (and children) "for the sake of the kingdom," parallel to becoming a eunuch "for the sake of the kingdom," is a cost that may be imposed by the demands of apostolic ministry.

There is evidence in the gospels that the apostles were viewed as exercising not only an evangelistic and missionary role but also in some sense a *priestly* one. The New Testament, of course, nowhere uses the term "priest" (*hiereus*) or high priest (*archiereus*) for ministers of the new covenant—understandably so, since in first-century Judaism "priest" denoted a descendant of Aaron who offered animal sacrifices in the Jerusalem temple.[46] There are, however, subtle indications that Christ intended the Twelve to serve as a new priestly leadership for a new Israel. Although space does not permit us to consider these in detail, a few indications will suffice.[47]

Mark 3:14 tells us that Jesus "appointed" (*epoiēsen*) the Twelve in a solemn manner to share in his redemptive ministry. The Greek word is literally "made" or "created"—a verb often used in the Septuagint for conferring a sacred office (cf. Ex 18:25; 1 Sm 12:6).[48] At the last supper, Jesus institutes and commands his apostles to repeat what would have been recognized as a priestly act—the offering of sacrificial bread and wine, now become his body and blood. In preparation for this, he washes their feet—a gesture that recalls the ceremonial washing that was part of the old covenant rite of priestly ordination (Ex 29:4; Lv 8:6). At Peter's objection Jesus responds, "If I do not wash you, you have no share with me" (Jn 13:8)—echoing an Old Testament formula used of the Levites, who have no "share" in the land because the Lord alone is their inheritance (Nm 18:20; Dt 10:9; 18:1–2).[49] Jesus' high priestly prayer in John 17 seems deliberately structured to parallel the priestly rites of the day of atonement in Leviticus 16. Jesus prays that the Father "consecrate" (*hagiazō*) the apostles (Jn 17:17, 19), echoing the words engraved on the gold plate of a high priest's turban, "consecrated to the Lord" (*hagiasma kyriou*, Ex 28:36).

But the most significant text, for our purposes, is in Matthew 12, where Jesus evokes two priestly precedents to justify his disciples' actions. This takes place on the occasion when his disciples are plucking heads of grain as they walk through a grain field on the Sabbath. When the Pharisees object that the disciples are violating Sabbath law, Jesus replies,

> Have you not read what David did, when he was hungry, and those who were with him: how he entered the house of God and ate the bread of the Presence, which it was not lawful for him to eat nor for those who were with him, but only for the priests? Or have you not read in the law how on the Sabbath the priests in the temple profane the Sabbath, and are guiltless? (Mt 12:3–5).

Jesus is recalling an episode in 1 Samuel, where David and his companions, fleeing for their lives from King Saul, seek help from Ahimelech, the priest on duty at the Lord's tabernacle. Ahimelech has nothing on hand but the "holy bread," the bread of the presence that was offered to the Lord every Sabbath and that priests alone could eat (Ex 25:30; Lv 24:5–9). But he offers David the bread on one condition: that he and his men have maintained sexual abstinence (1 Sm 21:4; cf. Lv 22:4–7). Only in this state of ritual purity would they be qualified for the proximity to God entailed by the priestly act of eating the holy bread. When David responds in the affirmative, Ahimelech consents. As Crispin Fletcher-Louis notes, "The way Jesus tells the Old Testament story, David plays the role of the priest who enters the sanctuary on the Sabbath to collect the old bread and distribute it to his fellow priests."[50] Moreover, Jesus' retelling places *himself* in the role of David and his disciples in the role of David's men who are granted a priestly privilege because they are on a sacred mission.

The second example Jesus invokes, not coincidentally, also involves the priesthood and the holy bread. The priests in the temple, he says, "profane the Sabbath" (Mt 12:5), so to speak, by doing the "work" of offering the bread of the presence as well as the other Sabbath sacrifices (cf. Nm 28:9–10). Yet they are "guiltless," precisely because they are carrying out the priestly duty of ministering to the Lord. Jesus suggests that just such a priestly exemption applies to his apostles, carrying out the priestly ministry of the new covenant. As the last supper account will make clear (Mt 26:26–28), they too will offer the "bread of the presence"—the bread that is no longer merely a symbol but the living presence of the Lord.

Although Jesus makes no direct reference to celibacy in Matthew 12, the priestly requirement of sexual abstinence is part of the contextual resonance of the passages he cites. When read together with his invitation to celibacy for the kingdom in Matthew 19, there is at least a suggestion that the apostles' ministry calls for the sexual continence that allows the absolute, undivided attention to the living God that was required of Israel at Sinai and priests on duty in the old covenant, now transposed to the Church where such priestly ministry is permanent rather than temporary. This does not mean, however, that the Twelve are in any sense envisioned as a reincarnation of the Levitical priesthood. Their ministry is not priestly in its own right but by participation in that of Jesus, the "great high priest" (Heb 4:14) who alone offers the sacrificial gift of himself that establishes the new covenant (Heb 9:15; 10:14).

CELIBACY AND PRIESTHOOD IN THE LETTERS OF PAUL

Turning to the letters of Paul, we find that the apostle also uses terminology that suggests an awareness of his apostleship as a priestly ministry—though again, one transposed to a completely different level than that of the Levitical priests.

In Romans Paul describes himself as a "minister [*leitourgos*] of Christ Jesus to the gentiles performing the priestly service [*hierourgounta*] of the gospel of God, so that the offering of the gentiles may be acceptable, sanctified by the Holy Spirit" (Rom 15:16). As Albert Cardinal Vanhoye points out, these are cultic terms that establish a close analogy between apostolic ministry and sacrificial worship.[51] Paul is envisioning himself as a celebrant who, through his work of evangelization, offers to God the holy lives of the gentiles who have come to faith in Christ and are sanctified by the fire of the Holy Spirit.[52] In 1 Corinthians, Paul even more explicitly compares his ministry to that of the Levitical priests: "Do you not know that those who are employed in the temple service get their food from the temple, and those who serve at the altar share in the offerings of the altar? In the same way, the Lord commanded that those who proclaim the gospel should get their living by the gospel" (1 Cor 9:13–14).[53] Although Paul is not speaking directly of the sacraments in these texts, the "offering of the gentiles" is intrinsically connected to them. It is precisely through baptism and the Eucharist that Christians become the "body of Christ" (1 Cor 10:16–17; 12:12–13), able to "present [their] bodies as a living sacrifice, holy and acceptable to God" (Rom 12:1).[54]

Paul views his celibacy—the renunciation of a legitimate good (1 Cor 9:5)—as stemming from his all-consuming commitment to his apostolic vocation (1 Cor 9:1–27). It is in Paul's desire to "please the Lord" (1 Cor 7:32) that his teaching on celibacy converges with his priestly understanding of his apostleship. As a "minister of Christ Jesus" (Rom 15:16) Paul passionately shares in Christ's spousal love for his church. As Christ "loved the church and gave himself up for her" (Eph 5:25), so Paul daily gives himself up for those whom he has "begotten" in Christ (1 Cor 4:15; cf. Gal 4:19). Like Jesus, he makes himself available to all and makes the cares of all his own. "Who is weak, and I am not weak? Who is made to fall, and I am not indignant?" (2 Cor 11:28–29). He "yearns" for his converts "with the affection of Christ Jesus" (Phil 1:8). He gladly suffers the hardships, fatigue, persecutions and "the daily pressure . . . of anxiety for all the churches" (2 Cor 11:28), so that he might make Christ's spousal self-donation visible and present to them in his own flesh. His celibate vocation allows him to image in a vivid way the ardent and exclusive love of Christ. But he does so by continually pointing not to himself but to Christ, whose slave he is (cf. 2 Cor 4:5). Paul is a true friend of the bridegroom, whose whole aim is to present the church "as a pure bride to her one husband" (2 Cor 11:2).

Two Counterarguments

Finally, our study would not be complete without considering two texts in the Pauline literature that at first glance seem to present strong counterevidence to the claim that the New Testament church saw a connection between celibacy and ordained ministry. The first is in 1 Corinthians 9, where in the course of defending his and Barnabas's conduct as apostles, Paul asks the rhetorical question, "Do we not have the right to our food and drink? Do we not have the right to be accompanied by a wife, as the other apostles and the brothers of the Lord and Kephas?" (1 Cor 9:4–5). The question rhetorically expects the answer "yes," implying that it was considered normal for apostles to be so accompanied. The Greek phrase translated "wife" (*adelphēn gynaika*) is literally "sister wife" or "sister woman." Most modern commentators interpret this unusual expression to mean a Christian wife,[55] although several Fathers of the Church saw a reference to a Christian unmarried woman.[56] But neither of these interpretations is entirely satisfactory. First, nowhere else in the New Testament is the expression "sister wife" used, even where the context would call for specifying that a wife be a believer (e.g., 1 Cor 7:2); the addition of the word "sister" would seem to be superfluous. Moreover, being accompanied by a wife would, for younger apostles, inevitably mean being accompanied by children as well (and thus being titled to material support from the local churches for them), yet there is no indication that such took place, nor that Paul expected the church to support entire missionary families. The second solution is even more problematic, since a situation in which an unmarried apostle (or, *a fortiori*, a married one) traveled with an unmarried woman (note that Paul speaks in the singular, not plural)[57] would have given ample occasion for scandal, yet Paul gives no suggestion of any scandal involved.

When this text is considered in the light of patristic usage—too often ignored in biblical exegesis—a different possibility presents itself. In the patristic era, the word "sister" in association with "wife" was the standard way of describing a wife with whom a sacred minister lived in sexual continence after ordination.[58] Although impossible to prove one way or another, it is at least possible that the New Testament church regarded Jesus' institution of celibacy for the kingdom as setting an ordinary standard of continence for ministers of the new covenant (whether they were single or married), as early church documents claim.[59] If so, then the meaning of Paul's phrase becomes clear: a "sister wife" is a wife with whom a minister of the gospel now lives in continence, having given up marital relations "for the sake of the kingdom."[60] Presumably these wives accompanied their husbands both to care for their material needs, like the women who followed Jesus in his public ministry (Mk 15:40–41; Lk 8:2; 23:49, 55), and to share in missionary labor, as in the case of Prisca and Aquila (Acts 18; Rom 16:3), and possibly Andronicus and Junia (Rom 16:7). This is how Clement of Alexandria, for example, interprets the text: "The apostles . . . took their wives around as Christian sisters rather than spouses, to be their fellow ministers to the women of the household, so that the gospel would reach them without causing scandal."[61]

The second potential difficulty arises from a phrase used three times in the pastoral letters, "husband of one wife."[62] This expression appears in the lists of qualifications for each of the groups of ordained ministers—bishops (1 Tm 3:2), presbyters (Ti 1:6), and deacons (1 Tm 3:12)—at a time when church leadership was transitioning from itinerant apostles to stable pastors of local churches. Candidates for these offices must be "the husband of one wife," that is, not married more than once.[63] At first sight this stipulation seems to undermine any link between celibacy and ordained ministry. But paradoxically, early church

legislation claimed it as evidence for the apostolic origin of clerical continence.[64] To see why this is so, we must first note that this
formula is not a general norm for Christians, since elsewhere
Paul allows for remarriage after the death of a spouse (1 Cor
7:39) and even encourages it in the case of young widows (1
Tm 5:14). Rather, the norm applies only to ordained ministers
and, in converse form, "wife of one husband," to a special order
of widows (1 Tm 5:9). Thus, although we cannot be certain, it
may reflect a situation in which ordained ministers were, like
enrolled widows, expected to remain continent, and a candidate who had married more than once was regarded as not
demonstrating the self-control required for this commitment.[65]
This was a common interpretation (though not the only interpretation) of "husband of one wife" for centuries, in both the
East and the West.[66] More significantly, as Ignace de la Potterie
has pointed out, "husband of one wife" alludes to the spousal
covenant between Christ and his Church (2 Cor 11:2), suggesting that sacred ministers are in a unique way called to image
that relationship.[67] Those who have married only once in their
lifetime show forth more clearly the exclusive love of Christ for
his bride the Church.[68]

CONCLUSION

Most of what scripture says about priestly celibacy is
implicit, not explicit. But taken together, the biblical texts form a
trajectory that leads seamlessly into the early church's discipline
of continence for ordained ministers,[69] which in the West gradually evolved into the requirement of celibacy for those ordained
to the priesthood. Jesus' institution of celibacy for the kingdom
was an innovation in salvation history—a new possibility that
can only be understood in the context of the "love of Christ
which surpasses knowledge" (Eph 3:19) and the superabundant
blessings of the kingdom that are now ours. Just as in the case
of Christ's abrogation of the ceremonial laws of Moses, it took
time for the full implications of this gospel innovation to unfold
in the church. Although at first the reasons put forth for clerical
celibacy often focused on the Levitical rules of ritual purity, a

growth in the understanding of biblical revelation has placed the emphasis on a deeper and more adequate foundation: on a priest's special share, as friend of the bridegroom, in the mystery of Christ the divine bridegroom and eternal high priest.

3

The Origins and Practice of Priestly Celibacy in the Early Church

Rev. Joseph T. Lienhard, S.J.

The emergence and development of the norm of continence and celibacy for the higher clergy in the early Church has a complex history, one that has been studied many times. In what follows, I wish to sketch this history briefly and perhaps to offer, in a modest way, one specific interpretation of that history, particularly in regard to its relation to asceticism and monasticism. As a conclusion, I will offer some basis for a theological reflection on priestly celibacy drawn from the writings of the Fathers of the Church.[1]

A few definitions of terms and axiomatic statements will clarify my approach.

Continence and celibacy are two key terms. Celibacy means being unmarried. Continence is abstinence from sexual relations and can be practiced both by celibates and by married people.

In the Code of Canon Law of 1983, canon 277, section 1, reads, "Clerics are bound by the obligation of keeping perfect and perpetual continence on account of the Kingdom of heaven, and thus are obliged to celibacy"; thus, the canon puts continence first and sees celibacy as a consequence of (*ideoque*) continence. The term "priest" for members of certain ranks in the clergy evolved gradually in the early Church. As various ranks of clergy developed, "bishop," "presbyter," and "deacon" stood out from other ranks, such as "subdeacon" or "lector." "Priest" (*sacerdos* or *hiereus*), in turn, was used only of bishops and presbyters.

Celibacy does not pertain to the essence of the priesthood, as the existence of married priests among Greek-rite Catholics makes clear. But bishops, even in the East, are required to be celibate, a fact that calls for further reflection.[2]

In light of these statements, my title may be misleading: historically, continence within marriage was required of the higher clergy before celibacy was. But that statement already involves us in the historical debate.

REVIEW OF THE LITERATURE

When the origins of clerical continence and celibacy are discussed, the matter is often called the Bickell-Funk debate, after two German Catholic scholars who exchanged a series of articles in the late nineteenth century. Gustav Bickell was the son of a Protestant canonist who converted to Catholicism, was ordained a priest, and taught at universities in Germany and Austria. Franz Xaver Funk, also a Catholic priest, was a professor at Tübingen. Both specialized in patristic studies. In 1878, Bickell published a learned article under the title, "Celibacy: An Apostolic Directive."[3] In 1879, Funk responded with "Celibacy: Not an Apostolic Directive."[4] In the same year, Bickell published a note, "Celibacy: Indeed an Apostolic Directive."[5] Funk's answer, in 1880, was "Celibacy: Not at All an Apostolic Directive."[6] While the authors might not win an award for creative writing, they formulated the central question for the modern dispute: does clerical continence or celibacy have an apostolic origin or not?

Books and articles on celibacy continued to be published in the first half of the twentieth century, of course, but the next great turn came at the time of Vatican II, when questioning the discipline of clerical celibacy increased markedly. The mass exodus from the priesthood (and in a few cases from the episcopacy) gave rise to a spate of spoiled-priest books, but they need not concern us here.

Pope Paul VI promulgated the encyclical *Sacerdotalis Caelibatus* on June 24, 1967. The Ordinary Synod of Bishops in 1971 reaffirmed the discipline of priestly celibacy.[7] The Eighth Ordinary General Assembly of the Synod of Bishops (September 30–October 28, 1990) treated "The Formation of Priests in Circumstances of the Present Day" and resulted in the apostolic exhortation *Pastores dabo vobis*, which also dealt with celibacy.

There was also some renewed historical research on the topic of celibacy after the council, often using historical criticism that disengaged itself from church dogma, for example, the work of Jean-Paul Audet, Roger Gryson, and Edward Schillebeeckx.[8]

The sex abuse scandal gave rise more recently to another spate of books, some of them filled with hate and vitriol, blaming the abuse on the unnatural demand by the Catholic Church of celibacy for its clergy. One such book is William E. Phipps's *Clerical Celibacy: The Heritage*.[9] In the introduction, Phipps wrote that "compulsory celibacy . . . has corrupted Christian theology and practice"; "the inhumane papal law of celibacy falsifies Christian core values"; and "required celibacy has resulted in immorality, criminality, female subjection, [and] hypocrisy."[10]

Passing over other recent books, one genre should be noted: histories of celibacy that maintain that clerical celibacy, or rather continence, has its roots in apostolic times attempts to defend, vigorously, the Bickell thesis. One is by Christian Cochini, a Jesuit, and was originally written in French and published in 1981.[11] Its title, in the English translation, is *Apostolic Origins of Priestly Celibacy*.[12] In 1993, Alfons Maria Cardinal Stickler published a small book titled *The Case for Clerical Celibacy*.[13] A third book, by Stefan Heid, a German priest who works in Rome, appeared in 1997.[14] The title of the English translation of Heid's book is *Celibacy in the Early Church: The Beginnings of a Discipline of Obligatory Continence for Clerics in East and West.*[15]

There is no place here to review all of Cochini's elaborate arguments, but his conclusion is this: "While the call to virginity was founded in the evangelical counsels, the discipline of priestly celibacy had its origins, as we have frequently seen, in a positive will of the apostles."[16] Heid reaches more or less the same conclusion:

> With a high degree of probability, then, the thesis recently advocated by Christian Cochini is correct: Already in the time of the apostles, or at the very least since the late New Testament period, a kind of obligation existed (and not merely an option) for ministers to practice lasting sexual continence—in short, a kind of celibacy law. Mere good intentions could not have provided the foundation for an institution, nor would they account for the unanimity that can be observed in the following centuries.[17]

The heart of Heid's argument is scriptural. The pastoral letters 1 Timothy and Titus prescribe that bishops, deacons, and presbyters should be "the husband of one wife" (*mias gynaikos anêr*). But St. Paul, in 1 Corinthians 7:9, writes that it is better for a widower to marry a second time than to burn and, hence, that if a widower cannot practice continence he should remarry. Heid reasons that a candidate for orders who is in a second marriage has proved he cannot live continently. From this it follows that married ministers were expected to practice continence with their wives from the day of their ordination.[18]

While I have sincere respect for Cochini's and Heid's careful studies, I cannot accept their conclusions as they present them. They apply a kind of reasoning to ancient texts that seems to me invalid. And further, they suppose that a sort of canonical legislation, and even central authority, existed at a period when the inchoative structures of the Church did not support such legislation or authority.

My own view is that, while the practice of voluntary continence or celibacy for the higher clergy began much earlier, the requirement of continence for the higher clergy arose in the West in the latter half of the fourth century and was brought about, in part, by the wave of enthusiasm for asceticism at that time. The ordination of monks, who were already committed to celibacy, grew more frequent. The practice of common life for the clergy, which had its roots in this era, also promoted continence or celibacy. And thus, higher clerics came to be expected to practice continence in marriage after ordination.

"THE HUSBAND OF ONE WIFE"

The text that is key to Stefan Heid's argument, "the husband of one wife," recurs three times in the pastoral epistles. I would like to examine the patristic exegesis of these key texts. I quote the Revised Standard Version: 1 Timothy 3:2 says of one who aspires to the office of bishop that he must be "the husband of one wife." 1 Timothy 3:12 says, "let deacons be the husbands of one wife." According to Titus 1:6, an elder should be "the husband of one wife." In the next verse, these elders appear to be bishops. As a parallel, a widow who is to be officially enrolled as such must have been "the wife of one husband" (1 Tm 4:9).

The Fathers of the Church proposed several different interpretations of the phrase, but few or none of them took it as implying obligatory continence for the clergy.

Some Fathers apply the phrase to marriage in general. Cyril of Jerusalem writes that a second marriage is better than fornication.[19] Clement of Alexandria uses the passage to praise marriage.[20] John Chrysostom says that, in this passage, Paul refutes heretics who condemn marriage.[21]

Other Fathers understand the text as discouraging or prohibiting second marriage for anyone. Ambrose comments that "one wife" applies to marriages contracted both before and after baptism; baptism washes away sin, not law.[22] Even Jerome writes that the bishop, married once, "can encourage monogamy and continence."[23]

Still other Fathers interpret the phrase as referring specifically to the clergy. For Theodore of Mopsuestia, bishops may
continue to exercise their marriage rights; he writes that a man
who is made a bishop will be content with his wife as the object
of his desires, although he allows a man married a second time
to become a bishop.[24] Others take the verse to mean that clergy
may not contract a second marriage. Basil the Great, in canon
12 of the canonical letters, writes that a second marriage absolutely excludes a man from the priesthood.[25] For Ambrose, a
man who marries twice is not guilty of pollution, but he is disqualified from the priesthood.[26] John Chrysostom is more restric-
tive: Paul does not mean that a bishop must have a wife but
that he may not have had more than one.[27] Tertullian mentions
that he remembered priests being removed from ministry for
marrying a second time.[28] The *Constitutions of the Holy Apostles*
laid down the general law: one marriage before ordination, no
marriage after ordination.[29] But none of these Fathers mentions
continence.

There are, however, some passages from the Fathers in
which "the husband of one wife" is understood as encouraging (or perhaps even requiring) continence on the part of the
higher clergy.[30] Eusebius of Caesarea, in the *Proof of the Gospel*
(written before the Council of Nicea), writes, "'For a bishop,'
says the Scripture, 'must be the husband of one wife.' Yet it
is fitting [*prosêkei*] that those in the priesthood and occupied
in the service of God should abstain after ordination from the
intercourse of marriage."[31] The so-called Ambrosiaster, writing
between 366 and 384 (during the reign of Pope Damasus) and
commenting on 1 Timothy 3:12 (the passage on deacons), writes
that, because of the small number of clergy in a local church
(as distinct from the time of the Old Testament), all deacons,
priests, and bishops "ought [*debere*] to abstain from intercourse
with their wives, because it is necessary for them to be available
daily in the church."[32] Ambrose, in the letter to the church at Vercelli already cited, also wrote that 1 Timothy 3:2 does not mean
that a bishop "may be encouraged by the Apostle's authority to
beget children; for he spoke of 'having' children, not begetting

them or marrying again."[33] Finally, Epiphanius of Salamis, writing circa 375, quotes the phrase "the husband of one wife" and comments, "But the Church does not admit as a deacon or a presbyter or a bishop or a subdeacon a man still living with his wife and begetting children, even if he is the husband of one wife, but rather him who keeps himself back from his one wife or is a widower. This is done especially where the ecclesiastical canons are properly kept."[34] These passages clearly indicate the direction in which the practice was moving but do not imply that continence after ordination was normative or obligatory.

Two points are important. The early Church took a dim view of serial polygamy on the part of any Christian.[35] The phrase "the husband of one wife" was generally taken to mean that a candidate for major orders must have married only once (and his wife only once), not as prescribing continence for major clergy. The picture that emerges is that a man married young and fathered a family; when he was ordained a deacon he continued to live with his family but no longer cohabited with his wife. The evidence for this picture comes mostly from the West. Threats of punishment from popes and synods show that this arrangement was difficult for many to live by.

The expectation that a married couple would live in continence after the man was ordained may seem unreasonable. But a passage in Origen's *Homilies on Luke* suggests that, in antiquity, a different attitude prevailed. Origen is commenting on the passage in Luke, chapter 1, that says, after she conceived, Elizabeth kept herself hidden. He writes,

> Even those who are joined in marriage do not consider every season free for intercourse. At times they abstain from the use of marriage. If the husband and wife are both aged, it is a disgraceful thing for them to yield to lust and to turn to mating. The decline of the body, old age itself, and God's will all inhibit this act. But Elizabeth had relations with her husband once again, because of the angel's word and God's dispensation. She was embarrassed because she was an old and feeble woman, and had gone back to what young people do.[36]

THE GRADUAL MERGING OF THE CLERICAL STATE AND THE ASCETIC IDEAL

Clerical continence or celibacy developed gradually in the first few centuries of the Christian Church. Two structures were joined: the higher clergy, namely, bishops, presbyters or priests, and deacons on the one hand, and the ascetical ideal on the other.

Pope Paul VI also took this view of the history of celibacy. In his encyclical letter on priestly celibacy promulgated in 1967, Paul VI presents a summary history of celibacy in the early Church[37]:

> Although it would be highly instructive to go through the writings of past centuries on ecclesiastical celibacy, this would take so long that We will let a brief account suffice. In Christian antiquity the Fathers and ecclesiastical writers testify to the spread through the East and the West of the voluntary practice of celibacy by sacred ministers[38] because of its profound suitability for their total dedication to the service of Christ and His Church.
>
> From the beginning of the 4th century, the Church of the West strengthened, spread and confirmed this practice by means of various provincial councils and through the supreme pontiffs.[39] . . . The supreme pastors and teachers of the Church of God . . . promoted, defended, and restored ecclesiastical celibacy in successive eras of history. . . . The obligation of celibacy was then solemnly sanctioned by the Sacred Ecumenical Council of Trent[40] and finally included in the Code of Canon Law.[41]

EMERGENCE OF THE CLERICAL ORDER

The structures of the higher clergy developed rapidly. In early decades, the Christian faith was spread by itinerant missionaries, often called apostles, prophets, and teachers. But the inadequacy of leadership by such men quickly became apparent.

They visited communities only occasionally and left them without stable leadership when they were absent. Further, different leaders might contradict each other; Paul can write of "false apostles," and we find the terms "false prophets" and "false teachers" in 2 Peter. The solution was local, stable leadership. There is some evidence that Jewish-Christian communities were governed by a college of presbyters; and Gentile communities, by bishops and deacons. By the time of Ignatius of Antioch, at the beginning of the second century, the two systems had begun to merge into government by one bishop (the monepiscopate), who was assisted by a college of presbyters who advised him and could take his place if necessary; the bishop was further assisted by deacons, who did not form a college but carried out tasks that the bishop assigned to them. This structure soon became standard throughout the Church.

THE RISE OF ASCETICISM

At the same time, asceticism was becoming a common Christian practice. Asceticism can be understood as freely giving up or surrendering something good and legitimate such as a rich diet, comfort in sleep, or marriage for something better, higher, and more spiritual. Ascetical practices are often seen as leading to higher states of prayer and to spiritual growth.

Jesus had recommended simplicity of life to the rich young man, if he wished to be perfect, when he urged him to sell all that he had and "come, follow me" (Mk 10:21). Jesus also taught that some of his followers could be "eunuchs for the sake of the kingdom of heaven" (Mt 19:12), a higher call for those who could accept it. He said, too, that his disciples would fast when the bridegroom was no longer with them (Mk 2:20; Mt 9:15; Lk 5:35), another sign of asceticism.

The earliest Christians took to ascetical ideals quickly and even eagerly. One of the more striking elements of second-century Christianity in regard to asceticism, however, is the Church's regular resistance to any attempt to make asceticism obligatory. The general term for any attempt to impose ascetical practices on all Christians is "Encratism," from the Greek word for "restraint." Many Encratites rejected marriage altogether. Some rejected the eating of meat. Some even substituted water for wine in the celebration of the Eucharist.[42] The teachings of many Encratites were rooted in dualism, that is, the rejection of the flesh as evil and the exaltation of the spirit as the only good. Orthodox Fathers consistently rejected Encratism: voluntary asceticism is a good, a great good; but ascetical practices are not to be made obligatory for all Christians. (There were exceptions, of course, such as the standard fasts on Wednesdays and Fridays.)

The problem with understanding the relation between clerical office and ascetical practices, especially continence and celibacy, is the scarcity of evidence for practices in the second and third centuries. Tertullian wrote *On the Veiling of Virgins*, in which he insists that virgins should wear a veil, that is, cover their heads. In the course of that work he refers to "men-virgins," saying there are many of them. They, of course, do not wear veils and thus carry their glory in secret.[43] Tertullian also attests that in his time, the early third century, many men in ecclesiastical orders lived in continence.[44]

Cyprian of Carthage, in his work *On the Dress of Virgins*, also mentions male ascetics. After quoting Matthew 19:11–12, on eunuchs for the sake of the kingdom, Cyprian quotes Apocalypse 14:4, a text rarely cited in this context: "Again, too, by these words of the angel the gift of continence is made clear, virginity is extolled: 'These are they who were not defiled with women, for they have remained virgins. These are they who follow the Lamb whithersoever he goeth.' And indeed not to men only does the Lord promise the grace of continence, disregarding women."[45] It is clear that there was an order of virgins in the Church, just as there was an order of widows. Like Tertullian, Cyprian is concerned principally with women; but he, too, mentions male ascetics.[46]

St. Augustine mentions the same: "I admonish the men and women who have embraced perpetual continence and sacred virginity to prefer their blessing in such a way that they may not consider marriage an evil."[47]

Thus we see an admiration for ascetical practices, beginning with the teachings of Jesus Christ himself. The practice of publicly professing virginity was well established by the late second century, and men as well as women voluntarily renounced marriage "for the sake of the kingdom." There is evidence, too, of voluntary celibacy or continence on the part of the clergy in these centuries. And further, it would seem more rather than less likely that clerics would adopt the ascetical way at least as eagerly as laymen and women did.

THE HIGHER CLERGY AND MONASTICISM

Beginning in the second half of the fourth century, a wave of enthusiasm for asceticism and the monastic way spread rapidly in the West. Soon after it was written (in 356), Athanasius's *Life of Antony* was twice translated into Latin. St. Augustine attests to its power: two young men read the *Life* and decided on the spot to become monks, breaking off their engagements (their fiancées became nuns).[48] Jerome supervised a community of women in Rome.[49] Ambrose oversaw a community of men outside Milan,[50] and he attests to groups of men living as monks on islands off the eastern coast of Italy.[51] The pagan Rutilius Claudius Namatianus saw a colony of monks on Capraria and found them disgusting.[52]

And monks also became clerics. Paulinus of Nola and his wife Theresia disposed of their enormous wealth in Gaul and Spain and founded a double monastery at Nola near Naples; Paulinus was ordained a priest on the way to Nola and later became its bishop. The people of Tours elected the monk Martin their bishop, and his biographer writes that soon many churches wanted monks from Martin's monastery as priests.[53] The island-monastery of Lérins off the southern coast of France served as a seminary for bishops in the fifth century.[54] In the East, the relation of monk to clergy was somewhat different: the monk had to leave the desert if a bishop wanted to ordain him, and many resisted, even to the point of mutilating themselves to avoid ordination. But many men in the East spent some years living an ascetic life and were then ordained priests and bishops; one thinks of Basil the Great of Caesarea, Gregory Nazianzen, and John Chrysostom, among others.

Fourth- and Fifth-Century Synodical Legislation

Beginning in the fourth century, we see a pattern of local councils, and bishops of Rome, requiring continence of married clerics. Almost all of these instances are from the West: Spain, Italy, and North Africa. Let me give a few of the best-known examples.

Canons from two local synods in the early fourth century are often cited in this regard. A synod in Elvira in Spain, around 303, forbade bishops, priests, and deacons to have relations with their wives and to procreate children, on pain of deposition from office.[55] The Synod of Arles (in Gaul) in 314 decreed that priests and deacons "should not cohabit with their wives, because they are concerned with daily ministry."[56] The authenticity of the canon of Elvira has been called into question;[57] if it is authentic, it would be an "outlier" for the early fourth century. The authenticity of the canon of Arles is also uncertain; it is one of six canons found only in a few manuscripts.

In contrast, evidence for the requirement of continence for the higher clergy becomes abundant in the late fourth century. Pope Siricius of Rome, writing to the bishop Himerius of Tarragona in 385, complains bitterly that he has learned that, in Himerius's territory, "many priests and deacons of Christ, a long time after their consecration, have procreated offspring, either from their own wives or out of shameful intercourse, and defend their crime with this excuse, that we read in the Old Testament that the faculty of begetting was granted to priests and ministers."[58] Siricius counters that all priests and Levites (deacons) are bound by an indissoluble law, that "from the day of our ordination, we hand over our hearts and bodies to the service of sobriety and chastity."[59]

In a letter he wrote to the bishops of Africa, after a synod held in Rome, Pope Siricius again stated that priests and deacons should not cohabit with their wives.[60] In the same paragraph, he quotes 1 Timothy 3:2, "the husband of one wife," and writes that Paul said this, "not about a man persisting in his concupiscence for begetting children," but "on account of future continence."[61] Here the pope interprets 1 Timothy 3:2 as commanding continence for the clergy.

A synod in Carthage, in North Africa, held in June of 390, decreed, "It pleases us that the bishop, priest, and deacon, guardians of purity, should abstain from their wives, so that chastity might be observed in all and by all who serve at the altar."[62]

Pope Innocent I, writing to Exsuperius of Toulouse in 405, dealt with the question of priests and deacons who have violated continence and begotten children. They are to be demoted from office, Innocent writes.[63]

These instances should make the pattern clear, if not more than clear. In the fourth century in the West, married members of the clergy were expected to live with their wives in continence.

Siricius also gives a schedule for ordination: if a boy wants to dedicate himself to the Church, he should be baptized before puberty and instituted as lector. If he lives an upright life and marries only once, and the woman he marries is a virgin, he remains a lector until he is thirty. Then he can be made an acolyte and a subdeacon, and then a deacon. If he serves well for five years, he may be made a priest. Ten years later, at forty-five, he may be ordained a bishop. Thus, obligatory continence would begin at thirty or thirty-five.[64]

MOTIVATION FOR CLERICAL CONTINENCE: RITUAL PURITY OR ASCETICAL IDEALS?

There is another topic that I can touch on only briefly here: namely, the motivation for clerical continence. I maintain that the motive was ascetical giving up something good for something better. Others, however, maintain that another motive was ritual purity: that sexual relations were considered unclean and that a man contaminated the night before by relations with his wife might not approach the altar. A recent book by David Hunter treats this topic at some length.[65] The problem, of course, is that many contemporaries find the argument from ritual purity repulsive, and it is hardly in line with the Church's teaching on the double end of marriage.[66] I would maintain, in contrast, that the controlling motive for clerical continence in the late fourth century was indeed ascetical, although the arguments in its favor were sometimes less apt than the ideal. The argument from ritual purity is not essential to the call to continence and celibacy; the ascetical ideal stands on its own.

THEOLOGICAL ASPECTS OF CONTINENCE AND CELIBACY

In the final part of this chapter, I would like to treat the theological and ascetical aspects of continence and celibacy as the Fathers of the Church presented them. The theological reflection on reason for priestly celibacy can be gathered under three headings: eschatological, ecclesiological, and Christological. The ascetical aspect primarily concerns human action, although theological principles lie behind it.

The Fathers of the Church wrote relatively little about clerical celibacy from a theological perspective. Most of what they said is found in treatises on virginity. These treatises, which deal primarily with women, also make occasional references to men who profess continence, and I will draw on these treatises as appropriate.[67]

Eschatological

The eschatological motivation for celibacy is the oldest one, attested by the words of Jesus himself in the gospels, when he speaks of "eunuchs for the sake of the kingdom of heaven," a phrase echoed in canon 277 on priestly continence and celibacy. Jesus taught that the kingdom is no longer a place for reproduction at all, as we hear in the passage about the woman with seven husbands: "When they rise from the dead, they neither marry nor are given in marriage" (Mk 12:18–27).

St. Cyprian of Carthage wrote, in his work *On the Dress of Virgins*,

> What we shall be, already you have begun to be. The glory of the resurrection you already have in this world; you pass through the world without the pollution of the world; while you remain chaste and virgins, you are equal to the virgins of God.[68]

St. Augustine wrote some sobering words against those who thought that celibacy was merely a way to avoid the troubles of marriage, rather than being an anticipation of the future kingdom:

> They are amazingly foolish, therefore, who think that the perfection of this continence is necessary, not because of the kingdom of heaven, but because of the present life, that is, because married people are distraught by so many urgent worldly cares, while virgins and celibates are freed from such affliction; as though it were better not to marry for this reason alone, that the cares of this life may be lightened, not because continence is of value for the future life.[69]

Ecclesiological

The ecclesiological grounding of celibacy sees the Church as the bride of Christ, and the priest as the concrete and visible representative of Christ to his bride. The bride is also a mother, who brings forth many children from the font of baptism. St. Augustine, again, writes beautifully:

> Since, therefore, the whole Church is espoused as a virgin to one man, Christ, as the Apostle says, how great honor her members deserve who preserve in their very flesh this which the whole Church, imitating the Mother of her Spouse and Lord, preserves in the faith. The Church, too, is both mother and virgin. For, about whose integrity are we solicitous if she is not a virgin? Or of whose progeny do we speak if she is not a mother?[70]

The celibate priest commits himself wholly to the Church, the bride, and by celebrating the sacrament of baptism makes her a fruitful mother.

Christological

The Christological argument for celibacy needs to be rooted in an understanding of Christ the High Priest. There is ultimately only one priest and one sacrifice: Christ the High Priest offering the one perfect sacrifice of himself on the cross. The Mass is the effective representation of that one sacrifice, and the priest who offers the Mass acts *in persona Christi*. St. Cyprian of Carthage put it beautifully:

> If Christ Jesus, our Lord and God, is himself the High Priest of God the Father and first offered himself as a sacrifice to his Father and commanded this to be done in commemoration of himself, certainly the priest who imitates that which Christ did and then offers the true and full sacrifice in the Church of God the Father, if he thus begins to offer according to what he sees Christ himself offered, performs truly in the place of Christ.[71]

St. Augustine speak of Jesus Christ himself as the model and ideal for celibacy:

> Certainly, the principal teaching and example of virginal integrity is to be observed in Christ Himself. Therefore, what more shall I prescribe for the continent concerning humility than He did?[72]

These texts from the Fathers hint at the foundations for a theology of clerical continence and celibacy. The celibate priest enters into a mystery, a mystery that is Eucharistic. Purely rational arguments and, even more, purely pragmatic arguments will never explain the call to celibacy. Priestly celibacy draws a man into the mystery of Christ, so that he says with John the Baptist, "He must increase, I must decrease," until he is nothing and Christ is all.

To speak of a theology of celibacy, however, involves a certain ambiguity. On the one hand, celibacy is not a dogma of the faith. To say, "Priests are required to be celibate" is not the same sort of statement as saying, "Christ is really present in the Eucharistic elements" or, "There are seven sacraments." Yet there is a true theology of celibacy, a way of talking about celibacy that treats it, not merely as a law or a discipline, but as one part of God's revelation of his great plan to save the world through Jesus Christ in the Church. This sort of theology requires a sense of metaphor, a sense for what is fitting rather than simply required, a sense for the whole Body of Christ.

Priestly celibacy is incomprehensible without Christian faith in the supernatural order. It is possible only for those who believe, with the creed, in "the life of the world to come." It is possible only for those who believe, again with the creed, "in one holy catholic and apostolic Church" that is far more than another social grouping in human society but rather the mystical bride of Christ. Priestly celibacy is possible only for those whose faith in Christ the High Priest sees faithful men as sharers in Christ's unique priesthood.

Ascetical Aspect

In the course of the fourth century, continence was more and more expected of clergy in the West. One may say, of course, that the Church was itself engaging in a kind of Encratism, of required asceticism. But no one was forced to join the clergy.

Pope Benedict XVI has written a beautiful paragraph on the Church's "very old" option for celibacy on the spiritual and ecclesial plane.

> The Latin Church explicitly emphasized the strictly charismatic character of the priestly ministry by linking priesthood (following in this a very old tradition in the Church) with celibacy, which quite clearly can be understood only as a personal charism, never simply as a quality of the office. The demand for separating the two ultimately rests on the idea that priesthood ought to be regarded, not as charismatic, but for the sake of the institution and its needs purely as an office that can be assigned by the institution itself. If you

want to take the priesthood so entirely under your own management, with its accompanying institutional security, then the link with the charismatic aspect found in the demand for celibacy is a scandal to be removed as quickly as possible. In that case, however, the Church as a whole is being understood as a merely human organization, and the security you are aiming for does not bring the results it is supposed to achieve.[73]

In other words, Pope Benedict suggests that celibacy keeps the Church from becoming a merely human institution, a corporation that hires the best resources. By asking for candidates who have the personal charism of celibacy, the Church confesses it is God who elects priests, not a corporation that hires them.

CONCLUSION

I would like to conclude with the words of St. Gregory of Nyssa, words with which he ends his treatise *On Virginity*, words he addresses to a priest:

Wherefore we would that you too should become crucified with Christ, a holy priest standing before God, a pure offering in all chastity, preparing yourself by your own holiness for God's coming; that you also may have a pure heart in which to see God, according to the promise of God, and of our Savior Jesus Christ, to whom be glory for ever and ever. Amen.[74]

4

Configured to Christ: Celibacy and Human Formation

Rev. Msgr. Michael Heintz, PhD

In the Rite of Ordination to the transitional Diaconate, the ordinand, on the cusp of his commitment to celibacy, is instructed that his celibate state will be "a sign of pastoral charity and an inspiration to it, as well as a source of spiritual fruitfulness in the world."[1] In contemporary culture, that sign is not always appreciated, and the value of the celibate commitment as an inspiration or motive is perhaps not sufficiently understood. To many of our contemporaries, be they Catholic or not, clerical celibacy can seem an onerous demand, a vestige of an earlier age that calls for a hasty *aggiornamento*, an accommodation to more modern sensibilities and mores. The relaxation of the discipline of celibacy in the Latin Rite, it is often suggested, might help to resolve the low numbers of priestly vocations and help to relieve the increasing demands placed upon priests. But

I personally think (I am not a sociologist so my reflections are impressionistic) that what is often called the "vocation crisis," the lower number of priestly and religious vocations in the past fifty or sixty years, is part of a larger crisis that afflicts marriage as well: a cultural crisis of commitment. Many contemporary people are terrified by permanent, lifelong commitments and the fidelity these entail. This might also help to explain the phenomenon of cohabitation prior to marriage: couples who cohabit do so most frequently I suggest, not merely because of lust but more out of fear, fear of the permanence of the marital commitment (there is, after all, no need to have the same address to be sexually intimate; my first pastor would characterize such relationships as *consummatum, non ratum*). Living together, so they think, will help them to confirm the commitment they are about to make. The evidence, of course, might suggest otherwise. Celibacy would seem, in our context, to make the priesthood less appealing, less attractive, and less marketable to one who may be discerning God's call. But too often, discussions and debates involving celibacy reduce the practice and the significance of clerical celibacy to sexual renunciation, making the necessary condition of its practice the sufficient condition for its understanding and significance. That is, the oblation of self, intrinsic to celibacy as understood in the tradition, is often reduced to the sublimation of concupiscence and sexual desire. In some ways this should not surprise us at all. Our culture so often reduces the mystery, the beauty—and, I would add, the inherent perils—of human sexuality to mere physiology, and as a result the temptation is to make the human formation for the celibate state a matter simply of the restraint and self-discipline requisite for the renunciation of sexual activity.

We need to remind ourselves that clerical celibacy is not merely the product of human effort, some kind of Stoic or Pelagian accomplishment of the moral order, but is a charism, a gift, and a grace, and in its character as sign, it cannot and should not be understood merely in terms of human formation. This is of course true in every form of the Christian life: each state of life requires particular efforts and specific commitments, but these efforts and commitments are also enabled and supported by grace, whether to marital fidelity, widowed continence, the chaste single life, or vowed religious virginity. While *sui dominium*, to use the language of the documents, is absolutely necessary for one who embraces celibacy, it is in itself insufficient; for fruitful celibacy, as a matter merely of will and unaided human effort, will not be possible. Further, as Augustine was very much aware,[2] there is an inherent peril facing those who embrace a life of sexual renunciation: a pride that insinuates itself in the heart of its practitioners and that can undermine the very virtue they seek to instantiate, because their celibacy then becomes precisely that, *theirs*, and thus a matter of personal accomplishment and a source of moral superiority, rather than a gift and living sign. For the priest, the grace and gift of celibacy as a sign and motive of pastoral charity will be muted if it remains merely the product of personal restraint and self-discipline, if he does not understand his priesthood, including his celibacy, in terms of configuration to Christ.

HUMAN FORMATION IN CHRIST

Human formation that is not linked intrinsically to spiritual formation fails, in fact, to be authentically human.[3] As Pope John Paul II taught so beautifully in his first encyclical, *Redemptor Hominis*, Christ not only reveals the fullness of God but also, simultaneously, by virtue of the Eternal Word's assumption of a complete human nature, reveals to us what it means to be authentically human.[4] In Christ, we see what we should look like, as it were, and we see in him the image—the image in which we are created—in its fullness, perfection, and beauty. We discover our identity precisely *in Christ*, and attempts to understand ourselves apart from this relationship established by our baptism will ultimately be deficient. In the formation of men for ordained ministry as priests, their developing self-awareness must never be severed from their relationship to Christ.

In the same way that Christ's human nature is the *organon* or instrument through which his Divine Person is revealed, encountered, and made salvific for us, it is the humanity of the priest that is to serve as a "bridge and not an obstacle" in drawing others to encounter Christ.[5] It is the human nature assumed by the Eternal Son that becomes, in the order of redemption, the condition of possibility for us to "hear, see, look upon, and touch" God himself.[6] Against the gnosticizing and docetic tendencies in the second and third centuries of the Christian era, representatives of the Great Church like Irenaeus and Origen would teach that it was the real and full humanity of Christ that was the condition of possibility for a visible and indeed tangible encounter with the Unseen God.[7] Christ's genuine and full humanity eternally united to the Divine Person of the Word attracted disciples and through his friendship with them revealed to them who they were called to be—they came to discover their identity "in Christ." In a similar way, too, the priest's humanity becomes, not an extrinsic vehicle, a matter of technique or method, but part and parcel, in fact, *the* expression, of his identity: the gift or grace of the priesthood, which like all divine gifts, is not meant to be clung to jealously but rather shared and given to and on behalf of others, is thus enabled, expressed, and made efficacious through his humanity. It should be precisely his humanity that draws others to encounter the priest as *alter Christus*, his priestly life and ministry enabled and enriched by the genuineness of his humanity, a humanity not "put on" or cloaking some deeper, more genuine identity, but personally making present and available that priestly identity to those whom he serves.

There is a direct relationship between the warmth, depth, and breadth of the priest's humanity and his pastoral fruitfulness, as grace builds upon and enhances his natural gifts. Thus, human formation is not about overcoming, transcending, or escaping what is most human, but of cultivating, nurturing, healing, and elevating by grace all that is authentically proper to our nature. This, in fact, is what makes a priest most effective—he is not a "superhuman," a man who has subdued nature or "bracketed" his humanity, but rather a man whose human nature is being renewed by a deeply personal and sacramental configuration to Christ, and it is precisely because of his humanity, under the aspect of grace, that Christ can work most effectively through the priest. The droves of folks who flocked to St. Jean Marie Vianney, for example, were no doubt attracted precisely by his gentle and gracious humanity, which then enabled his priestly ministry to flourish.[8] For the priest, "who he is" (identity) and "what he does" (function) are to become one and the same thing, just as by the time of St. Paul, the title Christ and the name Jesus—what he does and who he is—had already become instinctively yoked together in liturgical witness to this unity of person and work, of Christology and soteriology.[9]

The human formation of the seminarian must be geared to a personal encounter with and configuration to Christ, implicit in his baptism, but absolutely essential for his authentic human development and maturity. The goal of human formation, according to the *Program of Priestly Formation*, is to be more perfectly configured to the perfect humanity of Christ.[10] This, after all, is the kind of authenticity of which I speak: not the self-creation and self-assertion that characterizes contemporary self-understanding but rather recognition of the fundamental gratuity of the created order, including one's own existence and vocation, and the response of receptivity, communion, and gratitude that allows all self-awareness to become in some manner Eucharistic.

DIMENSIONS OF HUMAN FORMATION

As the late pontiff enumerated them in his postsynodal exhortation *Pastores Dabo Vobis*, the human qualities essential for the priest include the capacity to relate to others, an affective maturity, a genuine freedom, and the development of a strong moral conscience.[11] It is within the context of affective maturity that John Paul places his discussion of clerical celibacy, in the context where, according to the subsequent *Program of Priestly Formation*, the physical, psychological, and spiritual converge (evoking the biblical anthropology of St. Paul—we are body, soul, and spirit).[12] As a historical note, *Optatam Totius* had placed its treatment of clerical celibacy within the discussion of the spiritual formation of the seminarian.[13] The introduction by John Paul of the category of human formation should be seen not as removing, strictly speaking, reflection on celibacy from the realm of spiritual formation but rather as recontextualizing it more broadly; grace builds on nature. While celibacy is a supernatural charism, it must be rooted in the free choice of a healthy and stable humanity. While certainly not intrinsic to the priesthood itself (and we know this both as a matter of history and theology), celibacy is nonetheless very much part of what John Paul called the *logic* of the priesthood,[14] employing an aesthetic argument, a style of reflection we see in Athanasius and Thomas, for example, on the Incarnation, arguments not about strict logical necessity but about the particularly fitting or appropriate character of some measure of the divine economy.[15] Celibacy is particularly *conveniens* to the priesthood, John Paul suggests, because it enables an undivided attention to the Lord and to the apostolic ministry, it allows an ever-deepening configuration to Christ the High Priest, and thus—like all genuine oblative love that participates in Christ's agapic sacrifice—it is capable of bearing spiritual fruit.

One of the most helpful and important tools for assessing affective maturity and health is the psychological assessment conducted by a professional for or within a diocese or religious community in examining an applicant for studies. This cannot be undervalued as an important gauge and tool in assessing the human qualities and psychological maturity of the candidate. While never foolproof, it can help to identify pathologies as well as to indicate areas of needed growth and human development that can, through direction in both the internal and external *fora*, take place within a seminary or religious house. The psychological assessment of candidates is not my area of expertise; there are others far better equipped to address the issues related to such assessment.[16] But I do want to emphasize the importance of this dimension of screening candidates and offer gratitude to those professionals who assist dioceses, religious houses, and seminary formation staffs in this important work.

Central to affective maturity is the development of healthy friendships. One of the most important elements in the human formation of the seminarian (and the ongoing human formation of the priest) is the nurturing of a broad range of healthy relationships with men and women; ideally, a nexus of relationships should already be in place (at least in inchoate form) in the life of the candidate for studies. One would hope to see in the candidate a healthy and broad range of relationships emblematic of deep human sympathies and an openness to the breadth of human experiences. Integral to this is the capacity to relate well to married couples. For it is precisely through this witness of the total self-gift in marriage that the priest's understanding of and capacity for the self-gift, which is at the heart of his own celibate commitment, can be enriched and deepened. The seminarian needs to possess a deep respect and regard for the sacrificial love that marriage involves, not least to preserve himself from any sense of resentment for his own commitments and from wistful and overly romanticized fantasies about the nature of married life and love. This realization was captured in a beautiful way in the 1961 Pulitzer Prize–winning novel *The Edge of Sadness*, by Edwin O'Connor.[17] Written on the cusp of the council and yet delightfully devoid of the tensions that so often inform postconciliar fiction, the book is about a priest's relationship to a family with whom he was particularly close. At one point, late in the story, the priest, Father Hugh Kennedy, finds himself traveling in a car with a married couple he has known since long before they were married. While he sits in the back seat, he listens to the conversation between husband and wife in the front and he reflects,

> I saw that I had arrived at the border of the unknown land: the private preserve of husband and wife. Over the years I must have come to this precise spot literally a hundred times—I suppose most unmarried people have, but I think there may be a difference with priests, who by vocation are not only unmarried, but will always be so—and yet each time it never fails to jolt me a little, I imagine it's the sheer swiftness of the passage, for one thing: it always happens

in an instant. One moment you may be talking to an old friend, someone you've known as long as you've known anyone, someone you may even have known so well you would have sworn there was very little left to know, and then suddenly that someone will turn and speak to someone else in an entirely different way: a way so special, so direct and intimate that you wonder why words were used at all—it's as if the two had met head on and fused somewhere in midair before a syllable was spoken. And this is the point at which you realize that the old friend you knew so well has in fact dimensions you will never know—just as you realize that this way of speaking, this kind of encounter, which is so personal, so completely *shared*, is also something you will never know.[18]

What is particularly beautiful in this is that the author, himself not a priest, evokes an experience that I think almost every priest has had, and yet probably has not articulated nearly as well as O'Connor's description. His married friends are neither a threat to his priesthood nor an occasion for him to lament his celibacy. It is simply that he understands them, and himself, better because of this realization; it is an occasion of deepening self-awareness and gratitude. He encounters a kind of human intimacy (note it is not here a matter of sexual intimacy) that he will never know; yet he is not resentful but sees it as beautiful. In fact, earlier in the novel he had described his own experience of prayer, one that expresses a kind of intimacy known to all who truly pray but that must also be central to the unmarried priest, in which his deepest experience of intimacy is not with a spouse but with the Lord. He is describing the experience of learning to pray again during his time at the Cenacle, an alcohol-rehabilitation center for priests; as he relates it,

> I would suddenly become aware of a stillness quite apart from the stillness of the night. It was an interior stillness, a stillness inside me, a stillness in which there was the absence of all distraction and unrest, a stillness in which, quietly and without effort, I seemed to come together, to be focused and attentive, to be really

present, so to speak, a stillness from which it seemed
natural, even inevitable, to reach out, to pray, to adore.
. . . And this is what I mean by saying that slowly, but
at last, I came to terms with myself and with God.[19]

And as he indicates, this was a matter of deep self-awareness
made possible by that encounter in prayer, and as that issues in
gratitude, it becomes Eucharistic, because in recognition of the
gift, one offers oneself. Genuine self-awareness leads to self-gift.
The fictional Father Kennedy's recognition of what he calls a
"small and unsurrenderable core" that belongs only to God is
pivotal.[20] This is of course true of all persons, married or not.
In fact, the mistake one can make is to assume that human intimacy of any stripe can meet that deepest need. It is a temptation for the celibate to assume that the yearning for intimacy he
feels is necessarily a sign that he is called to marriage; this may
indeed be the case, but a more careful discernment is required.
For many married folks experience this same yearning and can
easily and sometimes wrongly assume this is a need that is not
being met by their marriage; in fact, it isn't because it can't. As
the Camaldolese writer Aelred Squire observed so shrewdly,

> A good deal of frustration in human relationships
> results from a failure to recognize that there is an ines-
> capable element of solitude in every human life, which
> not even marriage or the most intimate of friendships
> can evade. That is, indeed, something which each per-
> son must respect in themselves and in others as the
> most precious thing of all about them. It is something
> that cannot be given away, for in its ultimate depths
> there must be an aspect of every human soul which is
> virginal towards God. Most of the more terrible kinds
> of human unhappiness arise from a refusal to recog-
> nize this fact or the desire to evade it. It is the real root
> of each person's individual dignity, however, and the
> true source from which his greatest joy will flow, when
> the love of this unique love becomes fruitful at the
> level of his being which is accessible only to God. The
> Virgin Mother of God is thus seen as the type and ideal

of what each soul is meant to be, and not just those
who are formally consecrated to virginity.[21]

In some ways he is only expatiating on the Augustinian
insight that our hearts are restless until they rest in God by
whom and for whom they are made,[22] but this important truth
needs to be made very clear both to those preparing for marriage and to those preparing for celibate priesthood, for the
same reason: the mistake of thinking a human relationship,
and human intimacy (or for one already married, a *different*
human relationship, a *new* human intimacy), can meet our deepest needs and desires. As an aside, in preparing couples for
marriage, I will usually ask them if they pray together. Happily, some couples do indeed make a habit of praying together,
and this is of enormous benefit to their preparation for the sacrament. However, this question is met by many couples with
a look of deep perplexity, discomfort, and occasionally even
fright. For prayer, as they almost instinctively reveal by their
reaction, involves a kind of vulnerability and intimacy that is
quite intimidating. Here's the irony: many of those who react
this way are cohabiting or are already sexually intimate, and
this physical intimacy is apparently not nearly as intimidating as the prospect of shared prayer! And the celibate must of
course also be aware of emotional attachments that may never
become sexual (and so, technically speaking, may not violate
the canons of his celibate state) but that nonetheless become a
kind of surrogate for the intimacy he is to share with the Lord.

Just as the witness of married couples can and do enrich the
life of the priest and can serve to confirm and strengthen his
own vocation, conversely, it is the witness of the priest faithfully
and lovingly giving himself as a celibate to the Body of Christ,
the Church, that can offer to married couples a similar witness
of the agapic love to which they themselves are called within
their marriage, albeit expressed in a different way.

On a very practical level as well, the priest's capacity for genuine friendships with those whom he appreciates as his peers,
whether married, single, widowed, or his brother priests and
religious, is essential for a fruitful celibacy. They are essential

precisely because they will help the celibate priest avoid what might be called an "occupational hazard" of celibacy, a creeping solipsism, a kind of self-referentiality or self-absorption that may develop in one who does not, for example, have a spouse or children making demands on him and holding him accountable twenty-four/seven.[23] It is critically important that the priest has friends who know him simply as "Mike" or "Andy" or "John." I am certainly not suggesting the priest introduce himself to everyone as "just call me Mike" but rather that the seminarian and priest must have those who relate to him on a very basic level and in a very real way. These friends can and should have great regard for the priesthood but at the same time should know the seminarian or priest well enough to be able to challenge, and even cajole, him when necessary, holding him humanly accountable. It can happen that the seminarian or priest, under the guise of the celibate commitment, insulates himself from these most basic kinds of human relationships and the demands they make, and as a result never really be challenged on a human level. Real relationships make demands on us, and this is quite a good thing, as husbands and wives, who better each other all the time, can attest. However, within formation or priestly life, some might shy away from these demands or avoid them altogether, mistaking the promise or vow of celibacy for a kind of exemption from such human demands. This is actually an insidious kind of clericalism. The cleric can come to see himself in a kind of exalted position of dispensing or giving to others, a font of grace, but failing to remember that he, too, must be humble enough to receive from others and to reverence others, whether married, single, widowed, or vowed religious, as instruments of grace for the enrichment of his own priesthood. As a result of this kind of solipsism, personal eccentricities or idiosyncrasies can develop unchecked (and these may even work themselves out in a very public way within his celebration of the sacred liturgy), and as his self-awareness decreases or is skewed, his perspective becomes more and more limited, not only in regard to himself but also in regard to others. In such an instance, his humanity becomes less a bridge and more an obstacle for others in encountering Christ. Such idiosyncrasies hinder his ministry because people will stop short, so to speak, of encountering Christ through him. Instead, lacking the self-awareness that derives so often from our friendships, the priest will simply be promoting and drawing attention to himself; and precisely because he lacks self-awareness, he will likely be obtuse to this very fact. We can all think of a priest or two whom we have encountered in our life, a good man to be sure, but simply personally odd and who has apparently allowed no one close enough to him to say, "What is up with that?" As a result, he is less approachable, humanly less available, and his priestly ministry is less effective than it could be. Much of this could be prevented, I suggest, by maintaining a broad range of healthy human relationships—including some close priest friends and close nonpriest friends—where candid and honest conversation can regularly take place, where the demands of human friendship can become an occasion of grace, and in which the priest receives as much as he gives.

SELF-AWARENESS AND CONGRUENCE

The *Program of Priestly Formation* speaks about the "threefold process of self-awareness, self-acceptance, and self-gift."[24] The first is of course essential for the last. *Nemo dat quod non habet*: unless we have a genuine and honest sense of ourselves, we really cannot make a gift of ourselves. This is essential for the process of vocational discernment. It seems to me that there are two critical questions the seminarian must ask himself and must work out in conversation with his spiritual director as well as with his other formators in the external forum. The first is simply, who am I?; the second, what is the priesthood? Now, the first is not really a question of identity abstracted or apart from faith. In fact, it should be rephrased, who am I in Christ? since we are speaking about one who is already baptized, who has already been brought into the mystery of Christ; he is called, like all disciples, to discover his identity *in Christ*, how in particular he is called to share in the paschal mystery. Thus it is imperative that the candidate for ordained ministry comes to possess a deep self-awareness, a sense of his identity, his gifts and his limitations, his weaknesses and proclivities, and his potential for growth. That being said, the second question is equally important. For the second question is, what is the priesthood?—not as one might imagine it romantically or envision it as one might want it to be—but rather the priesthood *as the Church understands it*. This is discovered not only as part of the academic formation of the seminarian but also in lived fashion through the witness of the priest-faculty, the experience of pastoral formation, and spiritual direction. And of course integral to the Church's understanding of the priesthood in the Latin Church is celibacy. As the seminarian comes to answer each of these questions, a third emerges: are these two realities—who I am in Christ and what the priesthood is as lived in the Church—congruent? The answer to this alone is by no means the whole of discernment, because those entrusted with his formation are also making the very same assessment of him on behalf of the Church. These are, however, the most basic questions that he should be reflecting upon during his formation.

I used to ask those who might inquire about the seminary or the priesthood, prior to any formal application, a really basic question: do you think you can live the life?" But I have discovered upon reflection that this question is ultimately inadequate. It strikes me that there are a number of men who, while faithful to their vows or promises and, to that degree, are thus "capable" of living the life, nonetheless do so with teeth grit, simply *enduring* priestly life and its celibate commitment. It now strikes me that a better way to phrase or further qualify the original question is, do you think you can you live the life *with joy*? This qualification is actually central to understanding the question. The celibate life of the priest needs to be embraced and lived *with joy*. There are and will indeed be moments when one must "grit one's teeth," when concupiscence raises its distorted and distorting specter, and when specific human effort and self-mastery, with God's grace, will be called upon; but these are moments that are not defining, that do not undo or undermine one's more basic joy, joy made possible by the ongoing gift of self, literally embodied in the priest's celibacy and expressed most fully in his celebration of the Eucharist. There, at the altar, the priest's gift of himself to the Church can be taken up, as it were, and united to Christ's fully free gift of himself on behalf of his bride, the Church: "For this is my body, which will be given up for you." This celibate joy is not merely being upbeat or giddy, a human optimism or cheerfulness, but rather the fruit of Christ's Spirit, who liberates us from enslavement to ourselves. When we learn (counterintuitively, which is why it is graced) to dispossess ourselves of ourselves—when *my* priorities, *my* desires, *my* plans, *my* aspirations, *my* ambitions, and the prerogatives to which I cling so jealously are laid aside—that joy, the spiritual fruit of kenotic love, can then blossom.[25]

Optatam Totius duly emphasized the importance of both motivation and freedom in seminary discernment. St. Bernard of Clairvaux would ask those men who came to the monastery, "Ad quid venisti?" (Why are you here?).[26] Candidates for ordained ministry in the Church need to realize that integral to their discernment is celibacy. A seminarian of the Latin Church is not going to be called to the priesthood and at the same time not be called to celibacy; if not called to celibacy, he may be called to serve the Church in a number of roles, capacities, apostolates, or ministries but not as a priest. From day 1 in seminary formation, a vision of the priesthood needs to be offered, modeled, taught, and preached day in and day out in which the celibate commitment is part and parcel of that vision, and happily and joyfully so. Celibacy should not be presented or viewed as a drawback, a vestige of an earlier age, or something that (fingers crossed) may soon be changed. Once a healthy, vibrant vision of the celibate priesthood is offered—and again, the formational staff, the seminary faculty, is crucial in modeling such a vision—it must be freely and joyfully chosen, accepted, and embraced by the seminarian.

Formation for Chastity

Integral to seminary formation—and for all states of life—is the development of the virtue of chastity. In an oversexed age, chastity formation is an uphill battle. In the minds of many, the word "chastity" connotes restraint, limit, and repression, and is hardly thought of as a positive virtue. On a Catholic college campus, if there were two simultaneous symposia, one on social justice, the other on chastity, I suspect the former would garner a great deal more enthusiasm and attendance than the latter: understandably, the bright idealism and keen sense of social injustice common among undergraduates will likely make social justice much more attractive than chastity. In the imagination of the average collegian, the former sounds like "we're taking it to 'the man,'" and the latter more like "the 'man' is once again telling us what to do." While a caricature, what is unfortunate in this imagined scenario is that, in the end, *both* justice and chastity are virtues. The problem is that we often do not think of chastity positively as a virtue but merely as a restraint or a limit imposed on our freedom. However, at its deepest level, chastity is not merely about restraining carnal impulses; rather, it is a matter of vision or insight, about how one looks at oneself and the world. "Blessed," declares the Lord, "are the pure of heart: for they will see God" (Mt 5:8). Chastity is the virtue that enables us to see clearly, in fact, to see as Jesus sees; it enables true insight into ourselves, others, and the way things are. When one is growing in self-awareness and discerning God's will, there can be few things more valuable than clarity of insight. Recall the relationship between self-awareness and self-gift: one cannot properly make a gift of oneself if one does not possess self-awareness. This is why the discussion of chastity is also a very important part of marriage preparation, as couples discern their vocation to be husband and wife. They need to recognize that cultivating chastity in their own lives will enable them to see more clearly the will of God, to love each other more genuinely, and to prepare to give themselves to each other in marriage. Thus, the candidate for orders must be reminded that the way he lives as a seminarian—the habits, manner, behavior, patterns of prayer, and not least his commitment to chaste living—will be the way he lives as a priest. Grace builds upon nature, it does not evacuate it. Men who prorogue the full commitment to the life—whether in terms of embracing chaste celibacy; faithfulness to the sacraments and to prayer, in particular the Liturgy of the Hours; or the other elements of priestly life—and who await some extraordinary work of grace to suddenly enable and enliven these habits subsequent to ordination, are setting themselves up for disappointment. The Sacrament of Order indeed imparts the graces necessary to enable the priest to live his vocation but will not magically make up for what has not been cultivated in the order of nature. And while chastity obviously involves *sui dominium*, such self-mastery is not, as the *Compendium of the Catechism* points out, an end in itself, but it is meant to deepen human freedom and enable the gift of self.[27]

Further, the virtue of chastity can only take root and become strong in someone who is affectively mature. Affective maturity, precisely the locus in which Pope John Paul discussed celibacy in *Pastores Dabo Vobis*, is a sine qua non of chastity in the celibate state.[28] All of us—married, single, widowed, divorced, vowed religious, ordained, young, and old—have affective needs. We need to know we are loved, valued, and accepted. Balanced, healthy human relationships and a regular and solid habit of prayer must be staples for the seminarian and for the priest: the love of friends and the intimacy offered in prayer will serve well those needs. As mentioned earlier, human friendship is essential, but equally so is the intimacy offered in prayer, in deep personal communion with Christ, so that, on the basis of his own real experience of prayer, the priest can make St Paul's words his own: "I live by faith in the Son of God, who has loved me and given himself up for me" (Gal 2:20). When a seminarian or priest is not able to recognize the legitimacy of these affective needs or does not seek to meet them in a healthy way, it is likely either he will try to suppress them or they will perforce work themselves out in disordered ways: unhealthy emotional attachments, ecclesiastical careerism, alcoholism, pornography, acting out sexually, workaholism, or the double life of the nine-to-five priest, whose energies are spent racing through or escaping from his pastoral obligations to do the things he really enjoys and finds life giving. None of these can really meet or suppress his affective needs and are themselves merely poor substitutes or destructive spiritual narcotics. It is important to note that not all of these unhealthy or disordered ways of meeting these affective needs are explicitly related to violations of celibacy. However, a chaste and integrated celibacy in the life of the priest ensures that his affective needs are indeed being met in life-giving and ministerially enriching ways, in healthy relationships and in the habit of prayer. This is why the documents emphasize self-awareness and self-acceptance in relation to the self-gift that priestly life must be if it is to be faithful to Christ the High Priest, and to his bride, the Church.

A couple of generations ago, one of the watchwords among seminarians was "custody of the eyes." We may smile and think it quaint, but in an age when the images that impose themselves upon our vision are nothing if not relentless and are instantly at hand for those who wish actively to seek them out, there is great wisdom in the aphorism. For those who are seeking to cultivate the virtue of chastity, and certainly for those who are preparing to embrace celibacy, controlling intake and the self-discipline evoked in that old adage is no bad thing. In fact, one of the best antidotes to the hypersensual and hypervisual culture we live in is Eucharistic adoration. As the ancients knew well, and we seem to have forgotten, we are subtly but deeply shaped, affected, and formed by the objects of our contemplation. In stark contrast to the glitz and glam, the flash and fury of the images thrown at us by the various media, Christ reveals himself to us in the simplest of forms, in the seemingly most ordinary of elements, in a way that is emblematic of the entire divine economy, stooping down to us to show us himself, to give himself, and to heal our swelling pride by his own divine humility.[29] In an age when we face sensual sensory overload, to stop, to pause, to fix our gaze on Christ, and to have our imaginations shaped by him who gave himself for us should be a regular feature of seminary formation and of the ongoing formation of every priest.

CONFIGURATION TO CHRIST

The priest, by virtue of the Sacrament of Order, is configured to Christ the High Priest. This configuration, however, is a matter not merely of moral imitation—Jesus spent his time in service to others, proclaimed the justice of God, and lived a celibate life; therefore, those who follow him as priests must do the same, or so such a narrative might go—but also of *participation*. Functional theologies of the priesthood may rightly emphasize the importance of Jesus as exemplar for the priest, but this needs to also be complemented by a strong sacramental theology that understands the priest's participation in and personal configuration to Christ. In a beautiful and profound book that deserves to be much better known (and that is long out of print) titled *In the Redeeming Christ*, the French Redemptorist and biblical theologian François Durrwell writes of just what it means for the Christian to be *in Christ* and how the different forms and dimensions of Christian life express this relationship.[30] Language of configuration could undoubtedly remain somewhat vague or fuzzy, but Durrwell is quite specific about what this means. By virtue of the sacramental life, the believer is configured to Christ who is, in his words, "fixed forever in his redemptive act."[31] As he elaborates,

> Christ will never leave behind the immolation and that new life; his existence is fixed forever at the moment of the Redemption. The five wounds he showed his disciples are not merely the receipt for our ransom inscribed upon his body, but the wounds of a death from which he will never recover . . . the life of glory is a perpetuation of his death; the fire of the Spirit which consumes him keeps him as an eternal holocaust. The Lamb of God stands in glory and is surrounded by hymns of triumph, but he is still slain. . . . That ever actual glorifying action coincides with Christ's death, and thus keeps the Savior forever at the moment of his death to the world, at the high point of giving himself to the Father. . . . The Church, identified with Christ, finds this salvation of the Resurrection because

she is incorporated into the Savior, not in this or that moment of his life—Bethlehem, Nazareth, the roads of Palestine—not yet in a heavenly existence subsequent to the act of redemption, but in the act of Redemption itself. She is the Body of Christ in one precise, and henceforth, eternal, moment, in the moment when the redemption takes place, in the moment of his death on the cross, when Christ was glorified by the Father.[32]

All who are baptized are incorporated into Christ's Body, in this moment, fixed with Christ in his redemptive act; it is by sharing or participating in the kenotic self-gift of the Son to the Father that believers each in his or her way are enabled to make a gift of themselves in love. The celibate commitment of the priest in the Latin Church is a particularly fitting expression and eschatological sign of that gift of self that is distinctive to the priesthood and that anticipates here and now the life of the age to come.[33] But while celibacy is such a sign, it is also a stimulus or motive—it becomes for the priest the condition of possibility for an ever-deepening gift of himself on behalf of God's People. The renunciation of sexual activity inherent in celibacy is never an end in itself, never an ultimate accomplishment in which one can rest or be satisfied, a commodity or possession over which one preens, but rather a gift, charism, and grace of God that enables the priest more deeply to give of himself. It is a sign of the "end game," so to speak, but experienced in this age in a shadowy, incomplete way. It is not, here and now, and in the experience of every celibate, without its struggles, demands, and cost. But if embraced in humility and gratitude and lived in love and joy, celibacy becomes something at the same time that is life giving. Just as, according to Durrwell, Christ's glorification is simultaneous with his death (and this is quite Johannine—Jesus' hour and his glory are revealed coincidentally on the cross),[34] and just as Christ's death *is* the moment he gives himself to the Father, so too for the priest, configured to Christ by baptism and by his ordination, the renunciation inherent in celibacy is simultaneously a moment of gift, of fulfillment, and a source of deep joy, even if only inchoately so in this life.

In Christian marriage, the gift of self, made by each spouse, is expressed most fully and concretely in conjugal union. At that moment they are most fully who they are called to be as husband and wife; their fullest identity is made manifest as their words of marital consent, spoken once in time, are made flesh again; and they each can instantiate the Lord's words, "this is my body, for you." It is a participation in the paschal mystery distinctive to their vocation to marriage as they image and sacramentalize the love of God for his People, Christ's spousal love for his Church. So too for the priest, the moment when his identity is most fully expressed is at the altar, when, *in persona Christi capitis*, he makes the words of Christ his own—this is my body; this is my blood—and his gift of himself, embodied in and enabled by his celibate commitment, shares most deeply in Christ's gift of himself to the Father. Every other priestly work must derive from and be directed back to that moment, for it is precisely the paschal mystery, the dying and rising of the Lord, which St. Paul tells us we all carry about in our bodies (cf. 2 Cor 4:10), that gives shape, meaning, and purpose to every work, every prayer, everything the priest does, and everything he is. Perhaps those of you who are priests have had the experience of elevating the chalice and—depending upon the make and model, so to speak—have seen your reflection in it. It can be a revelatory moment: *this is your identity. This is who I am.* We priests, who by our ordination share in a particular way in that one paschal mystery, are, in imitation of and by participation in Christ, to give ourselves to, to pour ourselves out on behalf of, his bride, the Church. And like Christ's gift, it is and will always be a death, a renunciation, and a sacrifice. But it is also simultaneously the most fruitful, the most life giving, and the most beautiful of gifts.

5

The Virginity of Jesus and the Celibacy of His Priests

The Most Reverend Allen Vigneron
Archbishop of Detroit

In responding to the Church's call to take up the New Evangelization, it is essential that we have many worthy pastors "working in the harvest."[1] How can this come about unless the People of God encourage and support those who are called to the priesthood? And it is hard to image the Christian community fulfilling its vocational ministry unless we grasp again the worth of priestly celibacy. It is as a contribution toward this goal that I offer this chapter.

More specifically, the focus of my remarks is to help us think together about the virginity of Jesus as the basis, we might say the *arche*, of priestly celibacy. One would, then, be exactly on target to view this chapter as a guided reflection on the following passage from Pope Benedict XVI in *Sacramentum caritatis*: "The fact that Christ himself, the eternal priest, lived his mission even to the sacrifice of the Cross in the state of virginity constitutes the sure point of reference for understanding the meaning of the tradition of [priestly celibacy in] the Latin Church."[2]

In this one rich formulation, Pope Benedict, in his role as supreme pastor, testifies to three foundational convictions: first, the Lord Jesus lived his earthly life as a virgin; second, his virginity forms a unified whole with his priesthood; and third, the virginity of Christ the High Priest is the ground for the celibacy of his priests. It is my conviction that, as in all discussions concerning priestly celibacy, these three convictions must serve as guiding axioms.

With these three points distilled from Pope Benedict XVI serving as a strategic guide, in what follows I will develop my reflections on the relation of Jesus' virginity to the celibacy of his priests in three "moves." First, in what might be characterized in the schools as "positive theology," I want to look with you at the evidence that Jesus was, in fact—just as Pope Benedict affirms—a virgin. Second, in moving on to the level that can be called "speculative theology," I want to outline some of the elements that I see as basic for grasping that Jesus lived as a virgin. That will be the time to articulate points of connection between Jesus' virginity and the charism of priestly celibacy. Thirdly, I will suggest some of the tasks that fall to us, as men and women of the Church, to take up in our own spheres of competence in order to advance the New Evangelization by strengthening the agents entrusted with this important mission.

However, before I move to take up these three themes, I want to offer some observations that are more subjective in character. That is, I want to pause a moment to think with you about the nature of our own acts of reflecting together on the virginity of Jesus and the celibacy of his priests.

There are three basic categories of religious professionals I'd like to discuss: scholars, mostly in the guild of theologians; priests and others entrusted with the work of priestly formation, both before and after ordination; and bishops. Like most such taxonomies there are inevitable overlaps, a certain "hyphenating" in identities. For example, many are professors who have responsibilities in programs of priestly formation. While my own identity is that of a bishop, a pastor of the Church, I have also earned a rank in the guild of scholars and have worked full time in a seminary; however, it is as one especially responsible for the future well-being of the Christian community that I want to help all of us understand better how priestly celibacy is grounded on Jesus' virginity.

Regardless of the elements that go into establishing these identities, all are, each according to her or his own specific competence, members of the communion of saints, with responsibility for sustaining and advancing our communion. Those in each group depend on those in the other groups to fulfill the ends of our profession or vocation. We bishops need scholars and formators. Formators needs bishops and theologians. And theologians, because they speak, write, and think from within the communion of the Church, need pastors and those who form the pastors for the next generation.

So, while I am not a theologian, I aim my remarks to be theologically informed so they will offer solid stimulation to those who serve in the academy, so that you can further explore the link between the virginity of Jesus and priestly celibacy. Similarly, since my remarks come from one who has served full time in the ministry of priestly formation, I hope they will offer an apt resource to those of you who are charged with helping priests to flourish in the living out of their celibacy. We are here to think together for the good of the Church.

In sounding the theme of our diverse identifies and common mission, I am led to mention an identity that all of us, whether scholar, formator, or bishop, have in common. We are all teachers. Each of us has the august privilege of bringing to birth in other human beings, our students, those new habits of thinking and doing that weave themselves into the very fabric of their lives. Even if you who are professors do not have seminarians or priests in your classrooms, you teach them by what you write and publish and how you shape that part of the mind of the People of God we call theology. So, all of us are duty bound to arrive at an understanding and evaluation of priestly celibacy that will permit us in good conscience to hold up this way of life as a true good for those who are called to be priests and to hold up celibacy as a grace they can accept without fear. Not only bishops but all of us must be able to give priests and those who are on their way to the priesthood an honest and integral pledge that they are not in danger of slipping into the tragic sort of foolishness that would occur unless they were sacrificing their capacity for marriage to a good that was worth such a significant offering. I am convinced that understanding the celibacy of priests as a participation in Jesus' virginity is the key to our being able to fulfill this part of our mission in the Church. In this I see myself as following in the path marked out by Hans Urs von Balthasar, when he wrote that "the reasons for priestly celibacy [should be] presented as inseparably bound with the innermost of revelation and faith."[3]

JESUS WAS A VIRGIN

Having considered why it is important for the Church and for our own integrity as teachers to grasp and to explain the relationship between the virginity of Jesus and priestly celibacy, let us now take up the evidence that confirms Pope Benedict XVI's confession earlier, that "Christ himself lived his mission, even to the sacrifice of the Cross, in the state of virginity."[4]

Of course, the primordial witness for this affirmation about the virginity of Jesus should be sought in the New Testament: first, the evidence that Jesus did not marry; and second, the evidence that Jesus' unmarried state grew out of his mission and was coherent with his identity.

Any consideration of the historical basis for the Church's belief that Jesus lived his life and mission as a virgin must fairly begin by acknowledging that the New Testament does not explicitly affirm or deny Jesus' virginity. We do not possess a logion that is directly on point. However, the method of critical historical investigation is able legitimately to draw a conclusion about this matter through examination of the available evidence. In my review of the literature about the historicity of the claim that Jesus remained without a wife, I found the most solid historical-critical defense of this claim to be articulated by John Meier in his signature work *A Marginal Jew*.[5]

Meier carefully applies the criteria of critical historiography to the available data and concludes, "There are solid reasons for holding that Jesus was celibate," and "in face of the multiple relationships of blood and belief, both male and female, that the NT . . . report[s], the total silence about a wife or children of Jesus, named or unnamed, has an easy and obvious explanation: none existed."[6] And he ends his investigation with this passage: "To sum up: we cannot be absolutely sure whether or not Jesus was married. But, the various proximate and remote contexts, in both the New Testament and Judaism, make the position that Jesus remained celibate on religious grounds the more probable hypothesis."[7]

For Meier to characterize his findings about Jesus' virginity as "not absolutely certain" but "the more probable hypothesis" is, given the rigorous strictures of the historical-critical method, no small result. We can confidently maintain that there is no contradiction between what the Church affirms and what the evidence can bear.

However, beyond ruling out a contradiction between scripture and tradition, an attentive reading of the New Testament offers evidence for the virginity of Jesus in the form of its testimony that such a form of existence was, according to Jesus' teaching and practice, in full accord with the kingdom of God he was commissioned to inaugurate.[8]

We can, with the Italian theologian Angelo Amato, characterize this evidence as falling into two classes: "general," that is, those gospel texts that witness to Jesus' chaste detachment from the ordinary bonds of earthly life, and "specific," that is, Jesus' own explicit defense of the choice of the agents of the kingdom of God to forego marriage.

As for the general, according to St. Luke, already at the age of twelve Jesus asserts his freedom from the constraints of familial relationships for the sake of living out the consequences of his relationship with God the Father. Most of us can recite from memory the response of the young Jesus to his mother's reproach at having to search for him: "'Why are you looking for me?' he replied, 'Did you not know that I must be busy with my Father's affairs?'" (Lk 2:49). As Jesus makes clear in his response during his ministry that his mother and brothers want to speak with him, this freedom from the implications of natural family bonds involves not only his heavenly Father but also his followers. You recall his response: "'Who is my mother? Who are my brothers?' And stretching out his hand toward his disciples he said, 'Here are my mother and my brothers. Anyone who does the will of my Father in heaven, he is my brother and sister and mother'" (Mt 12:49–50).

In commenting on these passages Amato underscores their significance for understanding the virginity of Jesus and identifies their essential connection:

> From childhood on, Jesus considers himself free of family ties so as to bear witness solely to his communion in love with the Father in obedience to the mission he received. . . . [And] he creates new relationships, that of children of God, by his obedience to the will of his heavenly Father. His family is not based on blood relations. Chastity is the basis of this new relationship. Jesus belongs to everyone. . . . This is possible because he is chaste; his love is not partial but total.[9]

And, we can close the circle on this comment by adding that this chaste love for all is possible because it is communion in Jesus' total love for his Father.

To further deepen our appreciation of Jesus' own understanding of his virginal love for the community of sons and daughters that he came to establish for his Father, we shall consider briefly his title "bridegroom." Recall how, in the second chapter of St. Mark's gospel, when the Pharisees questioned Jesus about him and his disciples not fasting, he explains this in terms of his being the bridegroom.[10] In this he is appropriating to himself a divine title, the name for God as the spouse of Israel.[11] For, as Hosea confirmed, "It is the Lord who speaks— she [Israel] will call me 'my husband.'" (Hos 2:18). Jesus the virgin has no other love in this world than his love for the new people of the new covenant. He is a chaste spouse, who loves his bride with an undivided love.[12] It is a love of total self-giving, a love that courageously faces the bridegroom's being "taken way"—a formulation in which we are justified, according to N. T. Wright, in hearing a prediction of Jesus' passion and death.[13]

Jesus' logion about "eunuchs for the kingdom" offers us a more sharply focused insight into his own understanding of his virginity. In considering Jesus' words about those "eunuchs who have made themselves that way for the sake of the kingdom of heaven" (Mt 19:12), Meier affirms that we are on solid ground in thinking that here Jesus is offering a defense not only of his celibate disciples, those who "have left everything and followed [him]" but of himself and his virginity as well (Mt 19:27). For these disciples are "eunuchs for the kingdom," because they share Jesus' "total, all-consuming commitment to proclaiming and realizing the kingdom."[14] This is the kingdom within which, when it is established, husbands and wives will love one another faithfully and exclusively, as was intended "from the beginning" (Mt 19:8). So, we see that the virginity of Jesus is part of the fabric of God's kingdom; this nuptial love symbolizes and affects the renewal of nuptial love that is the fruit of the kingdom's coming.

In regard to other reliable witnesses to the virginity of Jesus, texts that, while not inspired, are authoritative, I will only offer a sampling.[15]

From among the Fathers of the Church, we should note testimony from St. Ignatius of Antioch and St. Augustine. St. Ignatius characterizes ascetics as those who practice continence "in honor of the flesh of Christ." St. Augustine, in *De sancta virginitate*, speaks of Jesus as "the Lamb who goes by a virginal road." In this context I would also like to cite St. Jerome's classic formulation of "Christus virgo."[16]

Both Aquinas and Bonaventure affirm that Jesus was a virgin. In his *Commentary on the Sentences*, St. Thomas affirms that Christ made no use of the male sex he took to himself at the Incarnation; he says that "Christ assumed a sex not in order to use it, but instead for the perfection of nature."[17] And in the

Summa theologiae, he writes that Christ "himself remained a virgin."[18] St. Bonaventure, in his *De perfectione evangelica*, says that the Christians who embrace virginity do so "in order to become like Christ the spouse, because that state makes virgins like unto him."[19]

I will bring to a close this subsection on the witness of the Doctors to Christ's virginity with one further citation, this one from St. Robert Bellarmine. In his exposition on the Epistle for Christmas Mass, Bellarmine sets up a parallel between "the ever-virgin Mother" and "the ever-virgin Christ."[20]

From the papal magisterium, I draw citations from two popes, one from before the Second Vatican Council; the other, after. In 1954, the Servant of God Pius XII, in his Encyclical on Consecrated Virginity *Sacra virginitas*, affirmed the virginity of Jesus when he wrote, "If priests, religious men and women, and others who in any way have vowed themselves to the divine service, cultivate perfect chastity, it is certainly for the reason that their Divine Master remained all His life a virgin."[21] In his 1967 Encyclical on the Celibacy of the Priest *Sacerdotalis caelibatus*, Paul VI likewise teaches that Jesus was a virgin: "Christ, the only Son of the Father, by the power of the Incarnation itself was made Mediator between heaven and earth, between the Father and the human race. Wholly in accord with this mission, Christ remained throughout His whole life in the state of celibacy, which signified His total dedication to the service of God and men."[22] We can see this teaching summarized in the *Catechism of the Catholic Church*: "Christ himself has invited certain persons to follow him in this way of life [virginity for the sake of the kingdom], of which he remains the model."[23]

The doctrine that Jesus lived his life in virginity has received its most authoritative endorsement by the Church's magisterium in the Second Vatican Council's Dogmatic Constitution on the Church *Lumen gentium*. In commenting on the vows of religious life, the Fathers praise the evangelical counsels because "they are able to more fully mold the Christian man to that type of chaste and detached life, which Christ the Lord chose for Himself and which His Mother also embraced." Here the council is recapitulating a remark found earlier in *Lumen gentium:* "The evangelical counsels of chastity dedicated to God, poverty and obedience are based upon the words and examples of the Lord."[24]

As a result of this research we can make our own the judgment of Bertrand de Margerie:

> Like the Resurrection, the virginity of Jesus is, at once and under different aspects, a historical fact and a mystery. It is not a solemnly defined dogma, but could well become one. One can and should say that it is taught by the ordinary and universal Magisterium of the Church as an incontestable truth, forming part of the deposit of Revelation: it is therefore a non-defined dogma.[25]

THE MEANING OF THE VIRGINITY OF JESUS

Assuming now that the Lord Jesus was a virgin, I would like to move on to consider the other two axioms: (a) there is an inherent connection between Jesus' virginity and his priesthood, and (b) the virginity of Jesus the Priest is the basis for priestly celibacy. To use the language of the schools, we are moving then from positive theology to speculative theology. More specifically, in this section we are engaged in that deepening of the understanding of the faith that the Fathers of the First Vatican Council said proceeds "e mysteriorum ipsorum nexu inter se."[26]

So then, let us consider the connection between Jesus' virginity and his priesthood, a connection Pope Benedict affirms but that, since he does not explicate it, becomes a task for us to take on.

Identity of the Gift and the Giver in a Nuptial Covenant

The key to identifying the link between Jesus' virginity and his priesthood seems to lie in the connection between Jesus as victim and Jesus as priest on Calvary, that is, in the identity between Jesus as *offertum* and Jesus as *offerens:* the sacrifice offered and the one offering the sacrifice. We speak concisely of this identity when we say, "Jesus offered himself on the cross."

Thus, an important step on our way toward comprehending the connection between Jesus' virginity and his priesthood is to grasp that the identity between *offertum* and *offerens* on Calvary is not accidental or merely happenstance. It has a meaning, a profound formal, personal significance. And the key to comprehending the meaning of this identity of *offertum* and *offerens* in Jesus on the cross is to recognize that the cross is the supreme expression of all covenantal sacrifice—the very point the Lord himself made at the Last Supper when he identified his blood as the "blood of the covenant," as we read in Matthew 26:28 and Mark 14:24—a covenant that is "new" according to St. Paul (1 Cor 11:25) and St. Luke (22:20) and "eternal" as we affirm in the sacred liturgy.

We make significant headway in articulating the connection between Jesus' virginity and his priesthood, through our focus on the identity of *offertum* and *offerens* in the new covenant sacrifice, when we recall that in salvation history the covenant between God and his people is essentially and irreducibly "nuptial" in character. In the covenants of both testaments God espouses his people.[27] This nuptial character is founded on two essential characteristics of these covenants: (1) they are always a communion of life, and (2) they are established by sacrifice—with each characteristic being essential for the establishment of the other.

The covenant between God and his people, like its paradigm, the marriage covenant, establishes a communion of life. At even a natural level such a covenant is "mysterious," since in this relationship one plus one becomes one (one communion)—a one that remains a two (the covenanted pair). Or as we read in Genesis 2:24, "The two . . . become one flesh." The covenant partners establish a new form of being; they have a common existence, and they act in common for a common end.

While in some ways these covenants are similar to a contract, they are strikingly different. The partners in a contract do not establish a communion of life, a common being. These covenants do not principally involve an exchange of goods but rather the exchange of persons. And it is precisely because of this fact that these covenants are established by a sacrifice.

The covenant of husband and wife is established by their mutual offering of spouse to spouse. The religious covenant, the covenant of God with his people, is established by a ritual sacrifice. In each case, by the vows that are made—either in words or in gestures—there is a mutual giving over of one's life to one's beloved.

In recognizing that these two nuptial covenants are essentially sacrificial, that is, established by the gift of self, we come to see two important consequences that follow.

First, because in these nuptial covenants each party makes an offering of the whole self, this relationship is exclusive. Its exclusivity follows from the gift of self being exhaustive. These covenants are exclusive because in each there is no more self for either partner to give to the other. Neither the man nor the woman and neither God nor his people have anything more to give. Therefore, there is nobody else to whom the gift of self can be made. This is the "originary" sense of the covenant restored as part of the mission of Christ and proclaimed by him in Matthew 19, where he speaks about how it was "from the beginning" (v. 8).

Second, because the covenantal sacrifice is the gift of self, the *offertum* and the *offerens* will always have to be the same. There is nothing extrinsic about these covenantal offerings. For husband and wife, and for God and his people, the gift and the giver are one. Any expression of this gift—whether in word or in ritual—only ever signifies but never substitutes for this total self-giving.

Jesus as Virgin and Priest

Having considered the identity of gift and giver in the offering that establishes a nuptial covenant, we are now prepared to articulate the intrinsic connection between Jesus' virginity and his priesthood. The new covenant relationship between Christ and the Church is, as St. Paul says so eloquently in chapter 5 of the Letter to the Ephesians, nuptial. The nuptial character of this relationship explains the necessity that, in the sacrifice of the cross that establishes this relationship, the *offertum* and the *offerens* are one.

Since this offering is of Jesus' whole self, it includes his sexuality. As Blessed John Paul II so forcefully reminded us in his "Theology of the Body," a human being is irreducibly sexual. Sexuality is not accidental, a sort of "add on" to one's being human. For a human being the giving of self is always the giving of the sexual self. Further, sexuality finds its true fulfillment in this gift of self. The nuptial meaning of the body indicates that not only does human sexuality shape what is given but also it essentially marks the act of giving. As Blessed John Paul II teaches, the law of the gift is inscribed in our bodies, that is, in our being sexual.

From the authoritative witnesses to the New Testament revelation, both in scripture and tradition, we know that Christ lived out his sexual identity as a virgin. He brought this virginal identity of his person to his paschal sacrifice. It was with a virginal love, a love only for his spouse the Church, that he gave himself to her and to no other. On the cross, as a virgin he gives his virginal self. "The Church's bridegroom comes as a virgin to his nuptial covenant with her, never having made a gift of himself to any other, one flesh with her alone—never [one flesh] with any body other than his Mystical Body, [giver] of no self-offering other than the one he makes to her in his Pasch."[28]

We are already well on our way to achieving our understanding of the relationship between Jesus' virginity and his priesthood, but there remains one more crucial step. We must consider the distinctive role Christ has in establishing the nuptial covenant with the Church. She, like him, is both giver and gift; however, each is not offering in the same way. As St. Paul reminds us in the Letter to the Ephesians, Christ's role in this covenant is as the "head," a role never ascribed to the Church (Eph 5:24).

To speak of Jesus as "head" of his body the Church is to underscore the truth that it is Christ who initiates the covenantal bond with the Church, and who always retains his preeminent authority in the covenant. While we can, in some sense, speak of the Church exercising a priestly function, since it, too, is both *offerens* and *offertum*, this priestly function is not primary but secondary; it is relative to Christ's. Christ is *the* one and only priest of the new covenant, because he, and only he, as the incarnate Savior, can establish and maintain the covenant by his offering of himself. For Christ, the two roles of head and priest of the covenantal communion are not joined accidentally. These are different aspects that are proper to the one same agent: Jesus, in taking the initiative to offer himself for the Church. Christ is the priest of the new covenant because he makes his self-offering as our head.[29] Christ fulfills this role as a virgin, with virginally exclusive love. He is all the more truly the definitive priest because he is a virgin; and his priestly act is the consummation of his virginity. It is in this way that Jesus' virginity forms a unified whole with his priesthood.

The Celibacy of Priests as a Share in the Virginity of Jesus the High Priest

On the basis of the insights we've shared about the relationship of Jesus' virginity to his priesthood, we can now move on to consider the third axiom I drew from *Sacramentum caritatis:* that the virginity of Christ the High Priest is the ground for the celibacy of his priests. By our thinking through what Pope Benedict means when he identifies Jesus' virginity as "a sure point of reference for understanding the meaning of the tradition of [priestly celibacy in] the Latin Church," we should better comprehend why being a priest and being celibate belong together.

For a convenient summary statement of the Church's conviction about what it is for a man to be a priest, we can look to the *Catechism of the Catholic Church*. Recapitulating the teaching of the Second Vatican Ecumenical Council found in *Lumen gentium* (nn. 10 and 28), *Sacrosanctum concilium* (n. 33), *Christus dominus* (n. 11), and *Presbyterorum ordinis* (nn. 2 and 6), the *Catechism* affirms two strategic points about the nature of the ministerial priesthood:

- First, the ministerial priesthood is a specifically distinct participation in the priesthood of Christ.[30]
- Second, his participation is not only accomplished by a sacramental rite but also establishes the recipient of the sacrament as himself a visible sign, a presentation, of Christ as "Head of his Body, Shepherd of his flock, high priest of the redemptive sacrifice, Teacher of Truth." And the *Catechism* goes on to explain that "this is what the Church means by saying the priest, by virtue of the sacrament of Holy Orders, acts *in persona Christi Capitis*" (CCC, 1548).

So, participation in Christ and presentation of Christ are the two parts of priestly being that are at the heart of what the Church knows about the ordained priesthood. Neither is detachable from the other, but each explains the other and accounts for it.[31] They are what some phenomenologists call "moments," that is, nondetachable parts of what it is for a priest to be a priest.

On the basis of the ordained priesthood as *participation* and as a *presence* in the priesthood of Christ the head, we can understand why being celibate belongs with being a priest. By the Sacrament of Holy Orders the whole person of the man ordained shares in Christ's priesthood and becomes capable of making that priesthood present.

To comprehend this "belonging together," let us be begin by recapping what we have seen earlier: it was as a virgin that Jesus consummated his work as high priest of the new covenant—making on the cross an exclusive and exhaustive gift of himself, inclusive of his sexual self—to the Church, his bride, by loving her "to the end." So by a life of celibate chastity the man who shares in and makes present the priesthood of Christ the head more deeply participates in and more clearly presents this total virginal self-giving of Jesus, which is the essence and foundation of his priesthood. Put simply, a celibate priest is more like Christ the High Priest, and so is and acts in ways that are more intensely priestly.

We find Pope Benedict XVI confirming this conclusion in *Sacramentum caritatis* 24, as he identifies priestly celibacy as part of that full configuration to Christ, which on a man's ordination day, becomes his agenda for life. As the Holy Father says,

> [Priestly] celibacy is really a special way of conforming oneself to Christ's own way of life. This choice has first and foremost a nuptial meaning; it is a profound identification with the heart of Christ the Bridegroom who gives his life for his Bride. A priestly life lived in celibacy [is] a sign expressing total and exclusive devotion to Christ, to the Church and to the Kingdom of God.[32]

And the Holy Father, while acknowledging the legitimacy of the traditions of the Eastern Churches, which do not require celibacy of their priests in the second order, goes on to point to these sister churches as confirming the practice of the Latin Church by their insistence that only celibates can be entrusted with the first priestly order, the episcopacy. We see the pope affirming that the link between the priesthood and celibacy, while not necessary in all cases, is essential, never accidental, and never the imposition by authority of an extrinsic qualification for the priestly ministry.[33]

OUR VARIOUS TASKS

In this final part of discussion, I would like to offers some suggestions about tasks we could undertake in our particular areas of competence, in order to strengthen within the whole Catholic community an appreciation for the meaning of the virginity of Christ, its relationship to his high priesthood, and its link with the ministerial priesthood, along with the practical actions that follow from such deepened appreciation.

Theology

Since any advance along these fronts will need to be built on a fuller comprehension of these graced realities, I will offer first some suggestions about tasks that could be usefully undertaken by members of the professorate in schools and departments of theology.

Christology

The most obvious specialization to speak about under this heading is Christology. It seems appropriate for every systematic treatment of Christology that aims for completeness to have a full exposition of the virginity of Jesus, offering the evidence from the sources of Revelation for this doctrine, articulating the level of authority with which the magisterium teaches it, and exploring the doctrine's meaning, especially through investigating how this particular mystery of Christ's life forms a coherent whole with the other dimensions of his mission and life—particularly with that concept or proposition that forms the foundational basis of the theologian's systematization of Christology: soteriology.

Further, because any systematic Christology will include in its synthesis an understanding of Jesus as the New Adam, the firstborn of the New Creation,[34] a thorough treatment of this central New Testament theme must discuss the sexuality of Christ, that is, his virginity and his role as the savior of human sexuality.[35]

Theological Anthropology

The further implications of the renewal of the human person accomplished by Christ are worked out in studies, lectures, and courses that examine the order of creation and how it is renewed and elevated by the redemption. In this sphere as well, the virginity of Jesus must be a topic of investigation. What Jesus Christ is by nature forms the paradigm for what all of God's sons and daughters become by the grace of adoption. This divinization of the human person in Christ Jesus cannot not involve human sexuality. As a consequence, the virginity of Jesus must be part of every systematic treatment of theological anthropology. And I am convinced that it brings a particularly rich source of insight into the work of those who aim to advance Blessed John Paul II's "Theology of the Body."

Mariology

One of the principal themes for specialists in Mariology is the perpetual virginity of the Mother of God. When the figure of Mary is examined from the perspective of her role as the primordial coworker in the mission of Christ, Jesus' virginity ought to serve as the basis for understanding hers, with hers being recognized as the participation that is fitting to her as the New Eve. When Mary is studied as the paradigm of the Church, considering Our Lady's virginity in relationship to Christ's would underscore that hers is a fitting response to the his initiative of love, lived "to the end" in virginity.

Theology of Holy Orders

Earlier in this chapter, in accordance with the authoritative teaching of the magisterium, I offered my own attempt to link the virginity of Jesus to his role as high priest and then to the priesthood as it is conferred in Holy Orders. I hold that any course or study on Holy Orders that claims to be complete must do the same.

Theology of Consecrated Life

Given the teaching of the magisterium that Jesus was a virgin and that his virginity is connected to his priesthood, I can identify at least two themes that will need to be examined in the theology of consecrated life: first, how the virginity of Jesus the High Priest is both like and unlike the virginity of those who make these vows apart from being called to Holy Orders; second—a more specific consideration of the first—how the vow of virginity pronounced by a man in a clerical institute is related to the celibacy he assumes upon his admission to Holy Orders.

Moral Theology

There are at least two ways the doctrine of Jesus' virginity can enrich moral theology. First, at the level of fundamental moral theology, with its exploration of Christian discipleship as a way of life based on one's absolute commitment to Christ, study of Jesus' virginity underscores that life in Christ is a share in the eschatological existence he has established by his life, death, and resurrection. And in moral theology's more specialized examination of the nature and requirements of chaste living, consideration of Jesus' virginity discloses the virtue of chastity, which permits excellence in living out human sexuality, as a participation in the virginal chastity of Christ.

Eschatology

In regard to eschatology, theology's examination of the "last things" ought to use the virginity of Jesus as a key to understanding how those who "make themselves eunuchs for the sake of the Kingdom" (Mt 19:12), like Jesus, already make present that age to come when there will be "no marriage or giving in marriage" (Mt 22:30). Ultimately, it is the virginity of Christ that will explain the meaning of human sexuality in the risen life.[36] The glorified body of the risen virgin Christ manifests the ultimate *telos* of the sexuality of all the blessed at their rising,[37] and discloses the relationship between sexuality's ultimate final end and its intermediate goal here below.

Apologetics

For those in the academy who engage in apologetics, there is much you can do to defend the virginity of Jesus against those who deny it, not only by challenging the historical reliability of any contrary hypothesis but also by calling into question the hunger in popular culture to posit a wife or consort for Jesus. In fact, as I've said elsewhere, I believe this second sort of defense of Jesus' virginity is more significant. I would frame the question this way: why is the plot of a marriage or a sexual relationship between our Lord and Mary Magdalene so attractive or so plausible to such a large audience? Or let us put the question in a turn of phrase taken from Cardinal John Henry Newman: why do so many people grant an antecedent possibility to the story line of a sexual relationship between Jesus and Mary Magdalene? Why does this idea seem to offer what they are looking for? My answer is that a nuptial relationship with a woman disciple would bleach out the eschatological dimension of Christ's life and ministry. This means that his Pasch would be left as a tragic accident that befell a decent "family man" and took him from his home before his time. In other words, this would tame Jesus Christ. Literally, it would "domesticate" him. And as a result, the Church would be understood as an intraworldly institution and not as a transcendent mystery.[38]

Thomism

Finally, for those who are Thomists, I would like to suggest this agenda item: an exposition of St. Thomas's observation in his *Commentary on the Sentences*, quoted earlier, that "Christ assumed a sex not in order to use it, but instead for the perfection of nature."[39] Such a study might with profit articulate out implications of the distinction Aquinas makes between the use of the sexual powers possessed as part of human nature and their unused possession as a perfection of that nature. Here one could explore the question of how a power that is unused is nonetheless perfected.

On the basis of what St. Thomas says in the *Commentary on the Sentences*, a scholar could go back and offer a rereading of all four articles of question 152 of the *Summa theologiae*, "*de virginitate*," to relate more comprehensively what Aquinas says there to his Christological affirmation in the earlier work.

Formators

For those whose first pastoral responsibility is the formation of priests, whether those in their care are seminarians or already ordained, here are some suggested tasks.[40]

Intellectual

In regard to intellectual formation, I will simply mention the obvious: priests need to have a thorough grasp of the three points from Pope Benedict: Jesus was a virgin, his virginity was integral to his priesthood, and his being a virgin-priest is the ultimate reason for priestly celibacy. These points must be part of the ordinary course in Christology at every seminary. To ask a priest to live a life of celibate chastity without giving him an understanding of the Church's teaching offered in capsule form by Pope Benedict is grossly irresponsible.

Personal (Human/Spiritual)

Of course, intellectual conviction about the meaning of celibate chastity for a priest, while a necessary condition for the exercise of that virtue, is not a sufficient condition. Virtues come from practice. To this end, those responsible for helping men develop the moral virtues required of a priest—whether in the internal forum or in the external forum—need to present celibate chastity as a participation in the grace of the virginal chastity of Christ the Priest.

In the period of discernment they will focus the prayer and reflection of seminarians on the question of whether Jesus is inviting them to share in this aspect of his being. After ordination, formators will challenge priests to remain faithful to the invitation once heard and accepted. Both before and after ordination, formators will reassure those they serve that the priestly virginity of Jesus guarantees to those whom he invites to share this grace that they will find in this form of existence the fulfillment of the aspirations to intimacy and paternity he has inscribed in their very being.

Those charged with priestly formation will hold those they serve accountable for living up to Christ's example of self-sacrificing love, heroic as it will be at times. And they will coach them in those practices necessary for faithfully living out in their lives the level of excellence in matters sexual found in the life of Jesus the virgin-priest.

Pastoral

Within the sphere of pastoral formation, the Church's faith about the virginity of Jesus the High Priest will not so much affect the skills to be achieved or further perfected as temper or intensify the sense of their exercise of these skills. A clear understanding of the priestly virginity of Jesus is essential as a motive for the well-ordered exercise of a priest's pastoral skills. A firm conviction about his celibacy being a share in the virginal love of Jesus the Priest will help to ensure that a priest's pastoral duties are not stultifying but made alive through their being performed as expressions of the pastoral charity that flows from the priestly heart of Christ, a charity no less ardent for being grounded in a virginal heart.[41] In this way, the most obvious reason for a priest's celibacy—namely, greater availability to serve—will be transformed from a merely pragmatic motive into one that touches the deepest level of a man's being. In the sacrifices a priest makes because of his participation in the agape of Christ the Priest, he finds that consummation of eros in divine agape to which Pope Benedict testifies so eloquently in *Deus caritas est*.

Bishops

Finally, here are some "action steps" for bishops.

Programs of Clergy Formation

Bishops need to be sure that those programs of clergy formation for which they are responsible are shaped in accordance with the Church's teaching on the virginity of Jesus the Priest. Each of us can attend to this matter in regard to the operations for which we are responsible or that we use for the formation of our priests and deacons. Further, bishops need to place the recommendations I offer above to those responsible for the formation of the clergy into revised editions of the "programs" that govern pre- and postordination in the United States.

Catechesis

Bishops should ensure that, in the intellectual formation of the catechists and teachers who work alongside our priests and deacons, the principal themes discussed above as worthwhile for theological study are covered. Certainly, at a minimum the Christology and Holy Orders courses should help our catechists understand the three axioms from *Sacramentum caritatis*. Such catechist formation is particularly important for those engaged in youth ministry, for it is on the basis of their sharing the convictions of the Church about priestly celibacy and its grounding that they will be able to effectively assist young men who are called to the priesthood to hear and answer this invitation. To further advance this goal, bishops should work to include a treatment of the priestly virginity of Jesus in the "High School Curriculum Framework" recently adopted by the U.S. Conference of Bishops.

Likewise, even those who teach adults need to be able to share the Church's teaching on the virginity of Christ the Priest and priestly celibacy with their students, for all the people of God need to know what the celibacy of their pastors means. In this way they can express their appreciation for the witness of their priests and offer them their encouragement. They too will be able to assist young men, especially the members of their own families, to consider the priesthood lived in celibacy as a personal blessing, a share in the existence of Jesus the Priest.

Episcopal Ministry

More generally, bishops need to make the Church's faith about the virginity of Jesus part of our preaching whenever this is appropriate. We must give forthright testimony to this doctrine at all times, especially when we speak about priestly celibacy. We need to witness to our own interior adherence to the Church's teaching and to the worth of the discipline of priestly celibacy. It would never be acceptable for us to respond to challenges about this teaching by shrugging our shoulders and saying that it comes from "headquarters" and there's nothing we can do.

CONCLUSION

As I conclude I want to set my remarks in a wider context, the context established by the direction in which His Holiness Pope Benedict is leading the Church today. He has called us to mark the fiftieth anniversary of the Second Vatican Ecumenical Council by committing ourselves once again to the task of evangelization, that is, to the New Evangelization—the fresh proclamation of the Good News of Christ the Redeemer to peoples and societies that once embraced it but have now grown tepid, perhaps even bored, with him and his saving grace. I believe that reappropriating the worth of priestly celibacy through a renewed affirmation of the virginity of Jesus the Priest is indispensable for the progress of the New Evangelization.

The good news is the news that Christ has risen, that he has conquered the worst of human disasters, sin and death, by the humble, all-embracing love with which he bore our sins and died our death. The good news our society needs to hear is that paschal love is victorious. The heralds of this good news now, more than ever, need to proclaim this paschal grace.

Von Balthasar was right to remind us that today as always Christ demands of the priests he sends to preach the Gospel "complete identification with [himself] the Lord who is sent by the Father to give his life for his sheep so that they may gain life, and who calls his follow men to participate in his sacrifice."[42] By living in celibate chastity, a priest proclaims this good news in his very flesh—the most powerful medium. It has ever been so. In our time, when both the high and the popular cultures are saturated with sex, the witness that celibate pastors make to the life-giving self-sacrifice of Jesus the virgin-priest, his "love to the end" on the cross, is at the heart of their service as heralds of the New Evangelization.

Finally, I direct us to von Balthasar for a word of encouragement to keep us from thinking that the good news has lost its power to generate paschal love in those who serve the paschal mystery or to enkindle a like response in those to whom they are sent:

> The history of Christian virginity . . . begins in Corinth, Ephesus and Rome, to mention only three of the most licentious cities of antiquity. Exactly there, where sin flowered most lushly—and the letters of the Apocalypse show us other telling examples—has Christian virginity its beginning. And if the virgins of earlier periods were respected while the celibates of today are ignored or scorned, let us once more point out that virginity and the cross, and hence disgrace, are closely related.[43]

In these words from this great theologian I find myself invited and I invite you, too, to take new heart. All appearances to the contrary, the good news proclaimed by our priest-pastors, both in their words and in their flesh, will not have lost its power, because the cross will never become impotent. Let us glory in Christ's cross and in all the manifestations of this mystery, including priestly celibacy, with the unshakable confidence that comes from believing that only if "the grain of wheat . . . dies will it produce any fruit" (Jn 12:24).

6

The Fatherhood of the Celibate Priest

Rev. Carter H. Griffin, STD

I n the course of these reflections on the fatherhood of the celibate priest I would like to make three points. First, I would like to specify just how a priest is a father and exercises his fatherhood. Second, I will argue that celibacy is ordered precisely to the exercise of that priestly fatherhood. Third, I will suggest three important implications of this thesis.

FATHER CHRIST

At the National Gallery of London there is a painting by Sebastiano del Piombo showing Jesus raising Lazarus from the dead. In this image, the Lord is reaching out his arm towards Lazarus, who is emerging from the tomb wrapped in linens, his sisters Mary and Martha and the crowd looking on, and Jesus' hand is in precisely the same posture as the hand of God the Father in Michelangelo's great fresco, the *Creation of Adam*, in the ceiling of the Sistine Chapel.

Whether Sebastiano intended it or not—*The Raising of Laza-rus* was painted only six years after the Sistine Chapel—he made a very important and theologically profound statement about Jesus' action in raising his friend Lazarus from the dead. As God the Father gave life to Adam, so Christ gave new life to Lazarus, as he gave new life to countless multitudes who came to him for mercy, truth, and healing, and as he continues to give new life in grace to countless more through his perfect act of love on the cross. Unwittingly or not, Sebastiano was harkening to an ancient undercurrent in Catholic thought that sees in Jesus not only the Son of the Father but also himself a father of a new and redeemed humanity.

It may seem a little jarring to call Jesus a father, but there is solid support for the idea in the scriptures and in the tradition. Adam himself, as we all know, is the father of humanity, the one commissioned by God to "increase and multiply" (Gn 1:22). St. Paul calls Jesus "the last Adam" (1 Cor 15:45), identifying him as the new father of humanity, the father in the order of grace, who has also been commissioned by God to "increase and multiply" a redeemed human race, to generate children for the kingdom of heaven. Many ancient writings take up the theme of Christ's fatherhood, from Justin Martyr to Irenaeus of Lyon to Athana-sius and Benedict, to name only a few. In Spain, I'm told, there is a "Christ the Father Cemetery," and in the Eastern Churches, it is not uncommon to hear prayers to "Father Christ."

There are hints of it in the gospels themselves. While I real-ize it is an idiom, Jesus very often used the affectionate term "children" when addressing his disciples: "Children, how hard it is to enter the kingdom of God!"; "Little children, yet a little while I am with you,"; "Children, have you caught anything to eat?"; and "My son, your sins are forgiven."[1] Most explicitly, in his ministry Jesus performs every action of the good father, pro-viding his disciples with food—both for their bodies and their souls—he guides and teaches them, and he protects them from harm. Above all, he gave them, and us, new life—the highest life of all—in the paschal mystery and prepared the way for our resurrection, our birth into eternal life.

Priest as Father

Christ is the Last Adam, the head of the Church and Father of a redeemed humanity, and the catechism reminds us that it is precisely to Jesus as head—that is, to his fatherhood—that a priest is configured in ordination (*CCC*, 1548–53). The celibate priest, then, is called "father" not from pious exaggeration or mere sentimentality but as a statement of fact. He is father because no man more than Christ is father.

In an age that has struggled with the very notion of priestly identity, this robust vision of the priest as essentially paternal offers us a refreshing and compelling way to grasp the priesthood. For the rest of this chapter, I will attempt to draw out the nature and the implications of this basic theological fact: that the priest's soul, configured to Christ the head, is thereby etched with the features of Christ's paternity. And it starts at the root of it all: in the very fatherhood of God.

Divine and Human Fatherhood

Jesus told his disciples, "Call no man on earth your father, for you have one Father, who is in heaven" (Mt 23:9). These words, so often used to argue for the unscriptural foundations of priestly fatherhood, are in fact its clearest witness. They reveal the profound truth that all human fatherhood—including that of the celibate priest—is grounded in God's paternity of the Eternal Son, his fatherhood *ad intra*, the ontological origin of all paternity in heaven and on earth, as St. Paul tells the Ephesians (Eph 3:15).

From this primordial fatherhood falls a cascading paternity into the created world. Jesus tells the Pharisees that God is the "God of the living, not the dead."[2] God delights in giving life; our natural world simply teems with it. The sheer variety of plants and animals attest to the fact that truly "God is the God of the living." I'm told that there are over seven thousand kinds of apples in the world. Cardinal Joseph Ratzinger, in *Introduction to Christianity*, described the wonderful superabundance of life that we see written in the book of creation. "Excess," he writes, "is God's trademark in his creation."[3] But there is one thing even greater than generating life; it is generating others who generate life. God is not only a generator but also a generator of generators, not only a father but also a father of fathers. And that begins the "cascade" into the created order.

St. Paul spoke of paternity in "heaven and earth," and as we trace the descent of fatherhood into creation, it is not a stretch to argue for a certain analogous paternity among angels through their intercessory prayer and through their protection. On the other end of the spectrum in the created order we can identify in animals a certain kind of paternity, though it is nonpersonal and so metaphorical. Midway between angels and animals are human beings, who enjoy the highest instance of fatherhood among creatures, generating—like God—rational persons, children destined for eternal life.

When God made Adam and Eve and inscribed into their being the call to be fruitful, then, he was inscribing a part of himself into humanity. Human generation is not simply the mechanism for procreation; it is sharing in the very life of God. This human paternity is found most immediately, most clearly, in biological fatherhood. In the communion of human persons in which a man and a woman generate a third, Almighty God enters into that union and creates something that did not exist before, something totally beyond their capacity to generate, an immortal, rational, human soul.

Wonderful as that is, however, human fatherhood does not end there. The man who conceives a child and then abandons him is not called a former father but an absentee father. The procreation of a child is ordered not just to its bare existence but also to its human development; not just to its generation but also to its natural perfection. In contrast to biological fatherhood, we can call this *natural* fatherhood, when a man provides for his child, guides and teaches his son or daughter, and protects his child from harm.

But the task of the human father goes still further. Biological and natural fatherhood are themselves ordered to the third and highest degree of human paternity: fatherhood in the order of grace—what we can call *supernatural* fatherhood. A human child, after all, is not born simply for this temporal life, not born only to enjoy the goods of this world, but also—and even more so—to enjoy the imperishable goods of heaven. We are born for eternal life. We normally think of human fathers and mothers as generators of their children's natural lives, but their highest claim to fatherhood and motherhood is as generators of their children's supernatural lives, through their prayer, sacrifice, teaching of the faith, setting an example of Christian discipleship, bringing them to the sacraments, forming them in virtue, and leading them to Christ.

There is a family I know whose son was recently born with severe physical defects. I don't know how long this child has for this earth, but I do know this family has showered this little child of God with love. He has been baptized and has received the prayers and sacrifices of his family and their friends. Whatever can be done to speed him on his journey to Christ has been done. There is no doubt in my mind that his parents have been shining witnesses of supernatural fatherhood and I pray they will rejoice one day with their son in heaven.

Supernatural Fatherhood of the Priest

And this brings us back to the priesthood. It is the great privilege of the celibate priest to dedicate his entire life to exercising this third and highest degree of human fatherhood, supernatural generation in the order of grace. Jesus, and therefore the priest, is a supernatural father in two ways. He represents his Father in heaven, his sacred humanity serving as a kind of icon of God. As he tells his disciples, "He who sees me sees the Father (Jn 14:9)," drawing those who confess him into the loving embrace of God's mercy. Jesus is also Father by his redemptive work, generating new life in the Church in the order of grace. So too the priest, configured to Christ, exercises supernatural paternity in both ways. He represents the mercy of God the Father and, instrumentally, generates supernatural life in the souls of his brothers and sisters.

In a moment I will suggest some ways that a priest concretely exercises this fatherhood, but before going any further
I would like to address an important objection that might be
raised. The other day, as vocations director, I was speaking to
an earnest young man who was convinced he could not have
a vocation to the priesthood because, though he likes the idea
of being a priest, he wants to be a "real" father. As you can
imagine, he was talking to the wrong person; by the end of our
meeting I think he was sorry he had said anything! But he is
not alone. However beautiful the thought of a fatherly priest,
most people—even of our own people, even priests!—are not
convinced that it is "real" fatherhood, genuine paternity. And
yet the framework I've suggested shows that the priest's paternity, if anything, is "more real" than any other.

It is said, for instance, that priests cannot of themselves
generate grace, supernatural life, in the souls of their people.
Certainly this is true; only God can do that. The priest's is an
instrumental paternity. But as we saw earlier, this is true of *all*
human fatherhood. Even biological fathers are simply coopera-
tors with God; sexual union can prepare the matter, so to speak,
but men and women in themselves have no more power to
generate human souls on their own than a priest can generate
grace. An immortal, rational, human soul can be created by no
one but God. God enters into that union and makes it fruitful,
and the same is true of the priest's ministry. His fatherhood, like
all human fatherhood, is instrumental, a cooperation in God's
activity, and yet, like biological fatherhood, not the less sublime
or "real." The priest's fatherhood, in short, is as genuine as it
gets: if the priest's is not true fatherhood, nor is any other!

Triple Munera in the Exercise of Fatherhood

Finally, before moving specifically to the contribution of
celibacy in this discussion, it is worth pausing to consider how
a priest concretely exercises his paternity. The Church already
offers us a framework in the triple *munera* of sanctifier, teacher,
and shepherd.

In the *munus sanctificandi*, the priest generates supernatural life by administering the sacraments. The priest or bishop bestows supernatural life in baptism, confirms and strengthens it in confirmation, heals it in confession and anointing, and directs it to the common good through Holy Orders and by witnessing matrimony. Above all, however, it is in celebrating the Holy Eucharist where the priest most visibly represents Christ the head, Christ the Father, in the liturgy and "generates" the Eucharist Christ in a way that echoes the Father's generation of the Eternal Son. The Eucharist is the source of supernatural generation in the Church, the food through which her children are nourished, and the highest exercise of the priest's fatherhood.

In the *munus docendi*, as teacher and preacher, the priest prepares his people to receive the sacraments, especially the Holy Eucharist, and helps to plant the seed of God's Word in their hearts. It is said that priests "father with their voice," and St. Paul gives us a powerful example of this supernatural paternity in his first letter to the Corinthians. "Even if you should have countless guides to Christ," Paul writes, "yet you do not have many fathers, for I became your father in Christ Jesus through the gospel" (1 Cor 4:14–15).

In the *munus regendi*, the priest fulfills the very fatherly functions of providing for his people and guiding them into truth and wisdom, leading them toward God. Every father must feed his children, and no one provides better nourishment than the priest, with the sacraments and God's Word, and through his prayer and sacrifice. Every father must teach his children and show them the way to happiness. No one more than the priest engages people in so many ways, so deeply touching their souls in moments of joy and sorrow, revealing to them God's love and mercy, with repercussions that last not just a lifetime but also an eternity. Every father must protect his children and no one more than the priest. Like Moses, he is called to stand in the breach, placing himself, like a shepherd, between his people and any danger that may threaten them, defending them from error and confusion within, and from threats without, even, if necessary, at the cost of his own life.

The priest's fatherhood, then, is not simply a conclusion of theology—it is the substance and lived experience of every priest's life. In reaching out to the marginalized, the poor, the suffering, the unborn, the sinful, the ignorant, and the lonely, he imitates the mercy of God the Father, of Jesus the Father, and in so doing realizes his own deepest vocation. Like all human fatherhood it is both procreative and perfective; it both initiates the life of grace and nourishes, purifies, heals, and protects it so it may thrive. The supernatural fatherhood of priests, paternity in the order of grace as sanctifier, teacher, and shepherd, is the joy and privilege of every priest, every day.

CELIBACY ORDERED TO FATHERHOOD

I would now like to pass to my second point, which is the role of celibacy in the exercise of this priestly fatherhood. The gift of celibacy, I believe, stands in brightest relief from the perspective of supernatural paternity.

In the Book of Genesis, when Abram was still childless, the Lord took him outside and said, "Look toward heaven, and number the stars, if you are able to number them. So shall your descendants be. And he believed the LORD; and he reckoned it to him as righteousness" (Gn 15:5-6). Abram strikes a beautiful image of the celibate priest who, though apparently childless, is called to generate innumerable children in the Lord. But there is another feature of this story that we sometimes miss. We usually think of Abram going outside, looking up into the night sky, and seeing the ocean of stars and being "unable to number them" because of their vast number. Six verses later, however, we read that "the sun was going down"! It was broad daylight when Abram looked up at the sky, and that's why he couldn't count the stars—because he couldn't see them! His faith, which was credited to him as righteousness, was the faith of knowing that God would produce from him countless children—children he couldn't yet *see*. He couldn't see the stars with the eyes of his body, but he could see his children with the eyes of faith. And this, truly, is an image of the celibate priest.

Earlier we traced the cascading fatherhood from God into creation, especially into men. We saw that the fatherhood of the priest, like that of Christ, both represents God's paternity and generates new life in the order of grace. The celibacy of the priest is a privileged way of living both aspects of fatherhood.

How does celibacy help the priest represent God the Father? St. Gregory of Nyssa and St. Gregory Nazianzen, and other Fathers of the Church, speak about God's paternity as virginal. While we typically think of "normal" generation as *mediated* generation through a physical communion of human persons, it is actually *celibacy* that more closely images the fatherhood of God, the virginal generation of the Eternal Son, and for that matter the virginal generation of the Church by the celibate Incarnate Son, and even the generation exercised by the Mother of Jesus and the angels. However beautiful human generation is—and it is beautiful!—the original "norm" of generation, of fatherhood, is actually virginal and is more closely represented by the fatherhood of a celibate priest.

Perhaps more concretely than this representative paternity, however, the instrumental paternity of the priest is emphasized by his celibate commitment. The celibacy of the priest who shares in Christ's headship is ordered to a radical, unmediated openness to God's will—St. Paul's "undivided heart" from First Corinthians 7:32–35—and a universal, generous love for his people. Earlier we evaluated this instrumental paternity of the priest through the triple *munera* of sanctifier, teacher, and shepherd, and the contribution of celibacy can be evaluated in the same way.

The Exercise of Celibate Fatherhood

In the *munus sanctificandi*, for instance, it has been argued that celibacy is particularly apt for the celebration of the Holy Eucharist. The sacrifice of the priest is reflected in his offering of the Holy Sacrifice of the Mass, as he stands in the place of the celibate Christ, as he echoes the celibate generation of the Eternal Son through his "generation" of the Eucharistic Christ.

More tangibly, perhaps, in the *munus docendi*, St. Thomas Aquinas teaches that celibacy is ordered to contemplation,[4] and it is through contemplation that a priest's preaching is nourished and made supernaturally fruitful. Every priest has had the experience of preaching from the overflow of his prayer and the impact that such preaching can have on others. If St. Thomas is right that celibacy can promote a contemplative life, then it can also contribute to the priest's "fathering with his voice."

It is in the *munus regendi*, however, that the priest's celibacy makes the clearest contribution. Celibacy offers him a wider scope of pastoral activity and facilitates his provision of the sacraments, intercessory prayer, and active works of charity. The Second Vatican Council describes celibacy as "a sign and stimulus for pastoral charity and a source of spiritual fruitfulness in the world"[5] and renders the priest "better fitted for a broader acceptance of fatherhood in Christ."[6] It opens his life to the needs of all his children, dilating his heart to embrace all his brothers and sisters. It is a visible witness to the dignity of human sexuality and an encouragement to human love that is healthy, faithful, and chaste. It prepares him to sacrifice on behalf of others, training him for the spiritual battle and even for martyrdom in defense of the faith and of his people. With recent events we now know that our religious freedom in this nation can no longer be taken for granted. We may or may not witness the martyrdom of blood of Christians in our country, but there are other kinds of martyrdom—we may have to sacrifice our reputation, our possessions, or maybe our freedom, to be faithful to the Gospel. And the detachment from these goods that celibacy fosters will help us prepare for it.

Celibacy, then, is ordered not simply to an imitation of Christ in his choice of celibacy. It is ordered to the priest's own ministry, to his fruitfulness in the order of grace, and to his fatherhood. It is particularly important to highlight this positive and compelling vision of celibacy in a skeptical age like ours that views celibacy, at best, as a regrettable relic of the past and stunting of human maturity, and at worst, as a cause of dangerous sexual aberrations.

Even those who support the discipline of priestly celibacy sometimes do so for reasons that are somewhat narrow. It may be, for instance, that celibacy is seen in the context of sacrifice alone, as an ascetical practice that contributes to the priest's own holiness. It may be seen as contributing to the priest's time, availability, and energy, permitting him to focus on his ministry in a way that few married men could. It may even be seen as a fitting way for a priest to be "married" to a virginal Church.

These explanations are valid as far as they go, but when understood to enhance the priest's very identity as a father in the order of grace, as coloring every fiber of his being and his priestly ministry, then celibacy becomes a rich source of human satisfaction, personal joy, and priestly fruitfulness. Celibacy is viewed no longer as a burden to carry but as a gift to treasure. As Pope Pius XII wrote so beautifully in his apostolic exhortation *Menti Nostrae*, by the law of celibacy "the priest, so far from losing the gift and duties of fatherhood, rather increases them immeasurably, for, although he does not beget progeny for this passing life of earth, he begets children for that life which is heavenly and eternal."[7]

THREE IMPLICATIONS OF CELIBATE PRIESTLY FATHERHOOD

In this final portion of the chapter, I would like briefly to address three implications of situating celibacy in the context of priestly fatherhood.

Normativity of Celibacy

The first is that celibate priestly fatherhood provides solid grounds to judge celibacy as normative for the priesthood and worth retaining as the discipline of the Latin Church. Unlike the evangelical counsel of virginity, which is ordered primarily to the priest's own holiness and the eschatological witness, the priest's celibacy is ordered—I believe like that of Christ—primarily to his ministry, his role in the plan of salvation. Just as Christ's celibacy was not absolutely necessary—he could theoretically have been married—so too the priest's celibacy is a normative, though not essential, dimension of priestly ministry. Like Christ, the priest is enabled through his celibacy to live his own supernatural fatherhood with greater efficacy and naturalness.

Celibacy thus finds its deepest logic not in the order of pragmatism but in the order of love; it is a form of sexual fulfillment in which the priest is able to give himself generously, fully, and fruitfully to his people in a particularly powerful way. Abolishing the gift of celibacy or making it optional, while theoretically possible, would forfeit one of the great gifts to the Church and render more challenging the fullest realization of priestly paternity.

Selection and Formation of Candidates for the Priesthood

A second implication of celibate priestly fatherhood is especially close to my heart as a vocations director and seminary formator. The compelling approach to celibacy as ordered to fatherhood helps to shape the selection and formation of candidates for the celibate priesthood. In a nutshell, if celibacy is a way of living paternity, then candidates for lifelong celibacy should first possess the qualities necessary for *human* fatherhood, and those in formation are to grow in the virtues required for generous, faithful, loving paternity.

Since the paradigm for supernatural fatherhood is found in biological and natural fatherhood, it is important that candidates for the celibate priesthood first have the desire, the capacity, the sexual and affective maturity, and the human formation to be holy and effective human fathers. One of the most fundamental questions that vocation directors and formators can ask themselves in evaluating a candidate is therefore, "Do I believe that this man would make a good father?"

It follows that one of the essential objectives of any formation program ought to be nurturing the virtues that would enable candidates to be not only good natural fathers but also exceptional ones. And this means choosing seminary formators who themselves are convinced of the celibate priest's genuine paternity and who possess the qualities and formation necessary to instill that conviction in their seminarians, and to help them live it out as priests. In addition, the competence of recognized experts on natural fatherhood would, it seems to me, be of immeasurable value when designing programs or guidelines for priestly formation.

As an aside, this framework of supernatural fatherhood is equally helpful in the formation of natural fathers, who are also called to exercise supernatural paternity in their own right. This is an aspect of marriage and baptismal preparation that is often, in my experience, glossed over. How beautiful would it be if every Catholic dad knew that his greatest responsibility in life was to engender supernatural life in the souls of his children, to help them get to heaven, and were given wise, practical advice to make that a reality!

Living Celibate Fatherhood

A final implication of celibate priestly fatherhood is an especially attractive vision of the priesthood well lived. I suspect that many of us would agree that the great enemy of the Church is not outside but inside—threats not from without but from the lukewarm, tepid priest within. I suspect, too, that most of us have seen the remarkable change that can come over a man who has just become a natural father, as his self-absorption gives way to a sense of responsibility and a beautiful desire to pour himself out for his wife and child. Fatherhood draws a man out of himself, widens his heart to envelop his new child, and braces him for the daily sacrifices needed to support his family. How many men do we know who toil away in thankless jobs, nourishing and sustaining themselves in their difficult work by gazing for a moment at a picture of their wife and children?

At one point in the gospels, we catch a glimpse of this in the life of Jesus himself. The Lord takes his disciples away for a period of rest—some rest that perhaps he wanted as well— but upon stepping out of the boat they saw crowds waiting for them, looking harassed and helpless, like sheep without a shepherd. Without another word, without hesitation, Jesus begins to heal, teach, and comfort (Mk 6:31–34). This is the heart of our master, the generous heart of a father. Celibacy can sometimes be viewed as a license for self-indulgent bachelorhood. When seen in relation to fatherhood, it is precisely the opposite, radically opposed to every form of narcissism, self-pity, entitlement, clericalism, and abuse of others. Taken seriously, I believe that celibate priestly fatherhood can be one path to genuine clerical renewal and reform, keeping our priesthood fresh, energetic, and vibrant. That's what celibacy can do, because that's what fatherhood can do.

St. Joseph: Model of Celibate Fatherhood

Sebastiano del Piombo, in *The Raising of Lazarus*, hinted at the power of Christ's generative love, his power to give life, and his fatherhood. Every priest is called to exercise Christ's own ministry of nourishing, healing, teaching, loving, and redeeming. He is called to be a father in the order of grace and to engender in others the seeds of supernatural life that will, please God, blossom into eternity. Every priest is privileged to share in this ministry, and the celibate priest, I believe, is invited to do so in a privileged way. When he lives his celibacy generously and deliberately as an expression of his supernatural fatherhood, it will be the source of untold fruitfulness in the lives of his people and immeasurable joy in his own.

Apart from Christ, perhaps the greatest human example of celibate supernatural fatherhood is found in St. Joseph. In describing the paternity of Joseph, Ephrem the Syrian proposes a striking image. It was thought in his day that male palm trees generated by covering the female palms with their shade, not by communicating any of their physical substance but by generating, as it were, nourishing, and protecting from a distance. This is the image St. Ephrem gives us of Joseph's fatherhood. He overshadowed Mary, herself the image of the Church, and her divine Son, with his love, pouring himself out for them, providing for them, and protecting them and in that love experienced his own deepest paternity, and his lasting, eternal joy.

St. Joseph's fatherhood was exercised in the order of grace, as is the priest's, who also finds his deepest joy in pouring himself out for the Church and for his people whom he loves so much. May each of us priests, like St. Joseph, exercise that celibate paternity generously, faithfully, and fruitfully, so that our title of "Father" may never be an afterthought but instead reflect our true selves: privileged fathers in grace who are ordained to generate countless children—more than the stars in the sky—brothers and sisters in Christ, with whom we hope to rejoice with God the Father, the Son, and the Holy Spirit, forever in heaven.

7

Beloved Disciples at the Table of the Lord: Celibacy and the Pastoral Ministry of the Priest

The Most Reverend J. Peter Sartain
Archbishop of Seattle

Something happened to me at Midway Airport the other day that has happened often since I was ordained a priest: walking down the concourse, I was approached by a woman who told me about a serious problem she was having in her marriage and asked if I would pray for her and her husband. I told her I would gladly do so, and immediately I sensed gratitude and relief on her face. She had a right to stop me and ask that favor, because as a priest I belong to her.

On Good Friday, I will do something I do only once a year: I will leave my episcopal ring on the dresser at home. The *Ceremonial of Bishops* indicates that on Good Friday "the bishop uses a simple miter, but not the ring or pastoral staff." That makes sense. After the Mass of the Lord's Supper on Holy Thursday, we strip the altars and sanctuaries of our churches and remove the Blessed Sacrament from its usual place. The paschal triduum jars us liturgically and emotionally to reflect on the Lord Jesus in the sleep of death. We feel his absence.

What was it like for Jesus' followers in the hours and days after his death?

When she found the tomb empty, Mary Magdalene anxiously reported to Peter, "They have taken my Lord, and I don't know where they laid him" (Jn 20:13). She was lost without her Lord.

Even before his death, Jesus had given a foreshadowing of what was to come. When the disciples of John the Baptist asked him why they and the Pharisees fasted but his disciples did not, Jesus responded, "Can the wedding guests mourn as long as the bridegroom is with them? The days will come when the bridegroom is taken away from them, and then they will fast" (Mt 9:15).

The *Ceremonial* explains, "In contemplating the cross of its Lord and Bridegroom, the Church commemorates its own origin and its mission to extend to all peoples the blessed effects of Christ's passion that it celebrates on this day in a spirit of thanksgiving for his marvelous gift"—the utterly selfless gift of his life for his bride, the Church.

Good Friday can be appreciated especially by widows and widowers. Does not all grieving contain a heavy measure of gratitude for the "marvelous gift" of the ones we have lost? It is their absence we notice, because they have become part of us. On Good Friday, the world felt lost while its Savior slept in death.

Every Good Friday, I am keenly aware that my paschal fast includes laying aside my episcopal ring; mourning with creation, I experience the death of the Lord in a particular way. Moreover, knowing that the ring symbolizes my spousal relationship in Christ with the local Church, I remember that, as a celibate priest, I, too, am to give my life for the sheep.

⌘   ⌘   ⌘

The "disciple Jesus loved" is an intriguing figure in the Gospel of John. He is never given a name, but it is clear that he had a profound friendship with the Lord. John refers to him directly or indirectly only about ten times, but the significance of his presence cannot be ignored. In art, he is often shown leaning into the side of Jesus, a sign of their closeness.

At the Last Supper (Jn 13), after Jesus announces that one of the apostles will betray him, Peter nods to the beloved disciple (who is "reclining at Jesus' side"), signaling him to ask who the betrayer will be. When Mary Magdalene finds Jesus' tomb empty (Jn 20), she reports the news to Peter and the beloved disciple. They hurry to the tomb themselves, but "the other disciple" outruns Peter.

After the resurrection, Jesus appears to his disciples at the Sea of Tiberius one morning at dawn, but they do not recognize him (Jn 21). Although they have caught no fish all night, he tells them to cast to the right side of the boat, and doing so, they haul in a great catch of fish. The beloved disciple then recognizes Jesus: "It is the Lord," he tells the others.

There is a particularly significant appearance of the beloved disciple in John 19. At the crucifixion, Jesus gives the beloved disciple to Mary as a son, and "from that hour the disciple took her into his home." By linking Mary with the beloved disciple, John is signaling something very important. Mary has been at the side of Jesus from the beginning of his public ministry at the wedding in Cana, embracing his mission and sharing his suffering. Now John reveals that Mary is given a role as the mother of all Christians, who are represented by "the one whom he loved." In that sense, Mary is a symbol of the Church herself. I would like to suggest that the beloved disciple is a model for priests, for we are called to be constantly at the Lord's side as his intimate friends, faithful disciples, and stewards of the house of God, the Church. At the post-Resurrection appearance at the Sea of Tiberius recounted in John 21, after Jesus asks Peter three times if he loves him, Peter spots "the disciple whom Jesus loved" following along and asks the Lord, "What about him?" Perhaps

Jesus' enigmatic response, "What if I want him to remain until I come?" can be seen as referring in a spiritual sense to us priests.

Mary and the beloved disciple remind us of the importance of intimate, faithful discipleship of the Lord. Jesus' profound love for them, and theirs for him, awakened in them such insight ("It is the Lord!") and fidelity ("Do whatever he tells you!") that they never left his side, especially at his darkest moments. They loved him and supported him, but it was from him that they drew their strength. It was for him that they gave their lives.

In this chapter I would like to enter the home of the beloved disciple and Mary, the Mother of the Church, and quietly savor with you the mystery of the Lord as revealed in priestly celibacy.

I will address the topic of the lived experience of celibacy in pastoral ministry through four of its aspects: (1) the priest's life of prayer; (2) priestly celibacy as an abiding sign of the living presence of Christ, an eschatological sign of the kingdom of God, and a necessary sign of contradiction for the world; (3) the priest as father to his spiritual family; and (4) priestly celibacy as a participation in the sacrifice of Christ and thus Eucharistic in its deepest reality.

THE PRIEST'S LIFE OF PRAYER

There can be no doubt that, after Jesus' death and resurrection, the discipleship of the beloved disciple and Mary was grounded in prayer. Artistic depictions of the beloved disciple leaning into Jesus' side offer a beautiful image of the source of the priest's strength for daily discipleship: prayerful friendship with our Lord. Evagrius Ponticus writes, "Breast of the Lord, knowledge of God; one who reclines on it (Jn 13:25; 21:20) will be endowed with theology." Evagrius's description of the beloved disciple as *theologian* is a beautiful image for us priests. Our faith in the Lord Jesus, our preaching and teaching, and our every pastoral task are fed by intimate familiarity with him, the kind that has its origin and sustenance in prayer.

While incarcerated in the Tower of London, St. Thomas More penned what he titled "A Godly Meditation" on the inside cover of his breviary, asking for the grace to "set the world at naught" in captivity. Among the litany of graces for which he prays, he asks to "lean unto the comfort of God, busily to labor to love him." He was seeking to be like the beloved disciple, who drew his strength from the Lord.

Celibacy is both a gift and a particular response to God's invitation to intimate friendship. It is thus inseparably linked to prayer, for in prayer we priests hear that invitation whispered repeatedly in our hearts. Both celibacy and prayer involve accepting the grace to be single-hearted. Without prayer, celibacy will be a burden and not the response of one who knows deeply that he is loved.

In the *Proslogion*, Anselm of Canterbury writes,

> O God, let me know you and love you so that I may find my joy in you; and if I cannot do so fully in this life, let me at least make some progress every day until at last that knowledge, love and joy come to me in all their plenitude. While I am here on earth let me learn to know you better, so that in heaven I may know you fully; let my love for you grow deeper here, so that there, I may love you fully.

Like prayer, priestly celibacy is participation in, and preparation for, heaven.

Certainly the busyness of priestly ministry makes it a challenge for us to be faithful to prayer. Much is on our plates every day, and discipline is an indispensable key. But we must go beyond discipline to depth, beyond routine to fire. We must be *theologians* in Evagrius's sense, mystics according to God's plan for each of us, and signs that the kingdom of God is here. The priest who lives his life steeped in prayer will be for those he serves a sign of *transformation*, *integration*, and *peace*. People will notice.

I hope to spend my priestly life in the house of Mary and the beloved disciple. I want to learn to do whatever the Lord tells me. I want to lean unto his comfort. I want to recognize him everywhere, however he chooses to come to me. I want to run breathlessly to his side, wherever that may be. I want to stay there, faithfully sharing his mission with Mary, Peter, and the beloved disciple. I want to know and love him so well that I will always speak clearly of him, so that others may know themselves as his beloved. He is my strength, and he will help me make some progress, every day.

PRIESTLY CELIBACY AS AN ABIDING, ESCHATOLOGICAL, AND NECESSARY SIGN

Priestly celibacy as an abiding sign of the living presence of Christ, an eschatological sign of the Kingdom of God, and a necessary sign of contradiction for the world.

Perhaps a story from the Desert Fathers will illustrate the power of a priestly life transformed and integrated by prayer.

> Three Fathers used to go and visit Blessed Anthony every year and two of them used to discuss their thoughts and the salvation of their souls with him, but the third always remained silent and did not ask him anything. After a long time, Abba Anthony said to him: "You often come here to see me, but you never ask me anything," and the other replied, "It is enough for me to see you, Father."[1]

Because the celibacy of Jesus is the model and origin of the celibacy of priests, when we speak of celibacy as an eschatological sign we intend that through it Jesus himself is revealed, as is the power of God's grace at work in the one who gives himself single-heartedly to Jesus alone. Origen called Jesus the *auto-basileia*, the kingdom in person. The prayerful priest, who lives his call to celibacy with single-heartedness and integrity, is an eschatological sign not because he is unmarried but because he belongs entirely to God and those God loves, and because he strives to allow God's grace to transform him so thoroughly that there is no dichotomy between his person and his message. He strives to live in conformity with the gift of holiness bestowed on him at ordination.

Pope Benedict writes, in *Jesus of Nazareth*:

> Jesus himself is the Kingdom; the Kingdom is not a thing, it is not a geographical dominion like worldly

kingdoms. It is a person; it is he. On this interpretation, the term "Kingdom of God" is itself a veiled Christology. By the way in which he speaks of the Kingdom of God, Jesus leads men to realize the overwhelming fact that in him God himself is present among them, that he is God's presence.[2]

In other words, we are to be a living sign of the presence of Jesus in the Church and thus in the world. It is as simple, and as challenging, as that.

As a sign in the *present*, consecrated and priestly celibacy points toward the *future* consummation of the Church's spousal union with Christ, which is already mystically present in every celebration of the Eucharist. The celibate priest, living his life and celebrating the sacraments *in persona Christi*, is a constant reminder to the Church that this world is passing away. We are called to live now as we shall all live then.

We live in an era that attempts to "see through" things, deconstructing and demythologizing them in suspicion that there is no ultimate reality, no ultimate truth. In such a climate, the concept of eschatological signs is dismissed as so much empty religiosity. C. S. Lewis addresses this modern inclination in *The Abolition of Man*, unmasking its emptiness:

> You cannot go on "explaining away" for ever: you will find that you have explained explanation itself away. You cannot go on "seeing through" things for ever. The whole point of seeing through something is to see something through it. It is good that the window be transparent, because the street or garden beyond it is opaque. How if you saw through the garden, too? It is no use trying to "see through" first principles. If you see through everything, then everything is transparent. But a wholly transparent world is an invisible world. To "see through" all things is the same as not to see at all.[3]

The priest, in the very act of fulfilling his ministerial call in the celibate state, reveals that there is something to see, *Someone* to see. That One cannot be explained away, and those who witness the integrated priestly life lived with love will be unable to deny that they have seen Someone—or at least, they will be unable to deny that they have seen a reality beyond their comprehension, a mystery they have yet to understand. If all they are able to do in the beginning is shake their heads in wonder, that is a start.

Simeon had told Mary in the temple (Lk 2) that her Son would be "a sign that will be contradicted" and that "you yourself a sword will pierce." Mary would also experience deeply the rejection of her Son, the pain of the cross, and the risen life.

Priestly celibacy is a necessary sign of contradiction in a world that seeks to make all things invisible, especially the truths of faith and their corresponding moral truths. Lack of discipline and order is more and more the societal norm. Priestly celibacy, lived with integrity and love, brings order—order not only to the life of the priest himself but also to those who experience the love of Christ through him. Such love, such order, stands out; it goes against the stream of many lives, drawing attention both to itself and, more importantly, we pray, beyond itself.

As a sign of contradiction, priestly celibacy is often misunderstood as an accusation or indictment. At times, the Church's discipline of celibacy evokes anger or annoyance from those who see it as an unnatural or unfair rejection of marriage. It is nothing of the sort. Much to the contrary, it is a sign of love, a sign that, when lived clearly, is a complement and elaboration of marriage. When it does meet rejection or ridicule, celibacy must be lived even more lovingly.

In a dialogue with priests during the vigil for the closure of the Year for Priests, Pope Benedict XVI said,

> It is true that for the agnostic world, the world in which God does not enter, celibacy is a great scandal, because it shows exactly that God is considered and experienced as reality. With the eschatological dimension of celibacy, the future world of God enters into the reality of our time.

It is for this very reason that the horrific scandal of the abuse of minors has been so devastating. However, it is also for this reason that, despite that terrible disgrace, most priests have realized that their parishioners still value them and, though they may pose serious questions even about priestly celibacy, are still drawn to the One who is present to them uniquely through their priests. Their priests are signs of the *autobasileia*, and even if they are unable to put such a reality into words, they instinctively know it is true. As Paul teaches about marriage, priestly celibacy, too, is a great foreshadowing, a sign that by its very power and depth cannot be ignored.

Still, in order for the sign to be clear and integral, the priest must be a man of prayer; he must learn to deal with temptation; he must daily seek prudence as an indispensable virtue; and he must live a life of renunciation.

Delving further into what clearly appears as a sign of contradiction in Christian life, Father Segundo Galilea links the search for happiness with Christian renunciation. He begins part 4 of *Temptation and Discernment* with the words of St. Ignatius Loyola ("The Three Ways of Being Humble," *Spiritual Exercises*, 167):

> Whenever the praise and glory of God would be equally served, I desire and choose poverty with Christ poor, rather than riches, in order to imitate and be in reality more like Christ our Lord; I choose insults with Christ loaded with them, rather than honors; I desire to be accounted as worthless and a fool for Christ, rather than to be esteemed as wise and prudent in this world. So Christ was treated before me.

Ultimately, Galilea points out, something that dehumanizes does not give happiness, and thus "to assure authentic happiness we renounce what gives apparent and fleeting happiness." What he says of every Christian life takes on particular significance in the celibacy of the priest. It is worth quoting Galilea at length:

> To be Christian all renunciation proceeds from a great love for the poor and crucified Jesus. It is the love to give oneself and be identified with Jesus that causes this happiness to be greater than the pleasure foregone, not renunciation or mortification for its own sake.

The joyful experience of giving something to God out of pure love, imitating very poorly the completely gratuitous gift of love God makes to us, is inexplicable for those who have not begun to fall in love with Jesus crucified. . . .

Christian renunciation is not inhuman. It situates us at the heights of humanism, whose essential premise tells us that we find human happiness in love, encountering greater happiness in greater love. The love with which we make the renunciation or mortification, growth in love for God, and the happiness it gives us are the most important criteria for discerning its legitimacy and appropriateness.[4]

There is indeed profound renunciation in the life of the celibate priest, and mortifications of various sorts can strengthen it. But the end result, contrary to common assumption, is not sadness but greater, deeper joy. Virginity for the sake of Jesus bears within itself an image of Mary, whose virginity, as Gregory of Nyssa suggests, produced great fruit:

O the wonder! The virgin becomes mother and remains virgin . . . the virginity does not prevent the childbirth, nor does the childbirth destroy the virginity . . . this seems to me to have been foreshadowed by the theophany of Moses . . . when the fire kindled the bush and the bush did not wither . . . so also here.[5]

Such a profound truth reminds priests that our celibacy *bears fruit* in a manner far beyond our understanding. What appears to be a contradiction is in fact the unveiling of a deeper reality: Christ in us. It also reminds us that in the home of the beloved disciple, we must observe Mary and cherish her presence as mother to our family, the Church.

THE PRIEST AS FATHER TO HIS SPIRITUAL FAMILY

I like to tell the parents of our seminarians that bishops, in partnership with seminaries, are in the business of *forming fathers*. If the seminarian undertakes priestly formation with love and authenticity, his parents will begin to notice that he is a better and more attentive son; his siblings, that he is a better brother; his nieces and nephews, that he is a better uncle—all of which are good indications that he will be a good father in the Church.

In *Catholicism: A Journey to the Heart of the Faith*, Father Robert Barron explains that God has forever been "in-gathering" his people, his family, those he formed after his own heart; and that the definitive in-gathering has happened through Christ in the Church.[6] I began with the image of the home of the beloved disciple and Mary, and I build on that imagery now with the important image of priest as father.

The celibate priest is called to be a sign of single-hearted commitment and active, selfless love for the Lord and those he loves. He is called to give himself so completely to God as his intimate friend and disciple, dedicating himself so completely to the up-building of the kingdom, that he allows God to teach him who his family is.

Jesus, speaking to the disciples as his "children" ("Children, how hard it is to enter the kingdom of God!" [Mk 10:24]), directs their attention not to the deprivation of giving all for the kingdom but to the gift of universal fatherhood—and the gift of the cross. Hearing this, Peter wonders how Jesus could expect more than they had already pledged. Could it be any more difficult?

> Peter began to say to him, "We have given up everything and followed you." Jesus said, "Amen, I say to you, there is no one who has given up house or brothers or sisters or mother or father or children or lands for my sake and for the sake of the gospel who will not receive a hundred times more now in this present age: houses and brothers and sisters and mothers and

children and lands, with persecutions, and eternal life in the age to come. (Mk 10:28–30)

The gift of celibacy means that, with the consuming love of the Father, the eyes and heart of the Son, and the unifying grace of the Holy Spirit, I must see everyone who comes to me as my immediate family—my brother, my sister, my son, and my daughter. When we committed our lives to Christ, we made a complete gift of ourselves—a sacrifice—to the Lord and the Church, as a husband to his spouse. We said, "I am yours." It is from that gift that our spiritual fatherhood arises, and one of the graces of celibacy is that in Christ our family expands to include all those to whom he sends us. No matter their age, race, culture, or language, they are our children—and they have a claim on us.

I cannot help but call to mind Paul's letter to Philemon. Philemon's slave, Onesimus ("Useful"), had run away; and during his absence he was befriended and converted by Paul, who sent him back to his owner with these words:

> I . . . urge you out of love, being as I am, Paul, an old man, and now also a prisoner for Christ Jesus. I urge you on behalf of my child Onesimus, whose father I have become in my imprisonment, who was once useless to you but is now useful to (both) you and me. I am sending him, that is, my own heart, back to you. . . . Perhaps this is why he was away from you for a while, that you might have him back forever, no longer as a slave but more than a slave, a brother, beloved especially to me, but even more so to you, as a man and in the Lord. (Phlm 1:9–16)

The context of Paul's words is not priestly celibacy, but the underlying meaning fits our context. Paul's relationship with Onesimus was that of father in faith, and it had changed everything for him, for Onesimus, and—Paul hoped—for Philemon. They were all "in the Lord."

The fact that our parishioners refer to us as "Father" is a daily reminder of our relationship to them in the Lord. At a time when so many families are bereft of fathers, our role is particularly important. We are fathers to young and old. I fondly recall kids playing in the gyms, fields, and parking lots of my parishes, for whom I was "Father Pete." But just as fondly I recall a seventy-year-old man, who burst into bitter tears in my office when he recounted how his father had mistreated him. He had come to his spiritual father for comfort and healing.

Many young people, having been reared in small or broken families, have never learned to live as a family, how to be brother or sister, mother or father. If they enter the seminary or formation for consecrated life, an important aspect of their formation is to be "fathered" and "mothered" by mature formators, so that through observing good models they will mature in a heretofore stunted feature of their young lives.

This aspect of maturing calls upon the deepest resources of the Church in identifying seminary staff members: generosity, self-sacrifice, humility, insight, perseverance, prudence, and holiness. Young men need to learn to be fathers who fall in love with God and those he loves, who learn to sacrifice with and through Jesus for the evangelization of the world. Young priests must be helped to see in the struggles of their early years that God is teaching them to love, that he is drawing out of them the depths of the resources he himself has given them, so they will love him and his family *from there*.

A pastor once asked me to meet to discuss his difficult parish assignment. British by birth, he had a particularly delightful way of expressing himself. He exploded with adjectives as he assessed the state of the parish and its members:

> My Lord, they are obstreperous, mulish, conniving, scheming, defiant, and fussy. They construct road blocks at every turn, they are not open to new ideas, they are cliquish and intolerant. They would object if the Lord Himself were their pastor. They treat me as if I were only the latest ox in a team bought to plow their fields. They keep a record of the length of my homilies and insist on the subjects about which I should preach. I cannot walk across the parking lot after Mass without one of them telling me what I ought do or not do. They thrive on rumor and pry into one another's lives as if nothing else in the world matters.

Pausing for a moment, he added, with a smile I will never forget, "And I love them!"

He did love them, and after a while, they loved him. In fact, it was precisely because of his love that the parish changed, and for the better.

One of the revered priests of the Diocese of Memphis (my home diocese) would never say a harsh word about another person. He surely had reason to be perturbed from time to time, but the most critical comment he would allow himself to make about another was, "I think he's a little nervous." He did not excuse bad behavior. He forgave it, because he loved his parishioners with the love of Jesus. As father of the family that was his parish, he created a home where respect, mercy, and forgiveness led the house rules.

Our role as fathers is to create a *home* for the family that is our parish and to love our parishioners as we would our own children. Would I give my life for them? Do I?

We bishops, vicars for clergy, directors of vocations, and seminaries are in the business of forming fathers.

PRIESTLY CELIBACY AS A PARTICIPATION IN THE SACRIFICE OF CHRIST AND THUS EUCHARISTIC IN ITS DEEPEST REALITY

When we priests kiss the altar, we are making a very public gesture in the presence of those gathered for the Eucharist; but at the same time kissing the altar is an intensely private gesture, an act of affection and surrender, an act of love and trust. Even more to the point, the priest's kiss of the altar is an act of identification: he is proclaiming to Christ, to himself, and to his parishioners that it is Christ the Priest who makes him who he is. We kiss the altar, which is a sign of the Lord himself, the sacrifice of Calvary, and the table of the Last Supper. Everything we do flows from the altar and back to it. The kiss symbolizes our daily embrace of the sacrifice of Christ as our way of life, for on the day of our ordination we were totally and irrevocably joined in character to him.

No matter the liturgical circumstance, we priests kiss the altar as a dramatic reminder of who we are and who we are called to follow, and as a proclamation to our parishioners that everything about us is *for them*. The gesture has become so important to me that I begin and end my holy hour by kissing the altar. Doing so reminds me that as a priest I both pray and minister *from the cross*.

Serving *in persona Christi* means we are not just envoys with a message, not just deliverers of the fruit, but ministers in him *from the cross*. Our people look to us as to Christ, and they have a right to do so. From the cross, however, the Lord has asked us to bear it with him, we are called to serve them in a loving, self-offering embrace. We are *for you*, we might say, because we are *in him*. A life of priestly ministry entails loving from the cross in one unfolding and lifelong act of self-oblation. That is why the Eucharist will always stand at the center of our lives.

A bishop's ministry must never be reduced to mere administration. This was a point of focus for the bishops gathered for the Tenth Ordinary General Assembly of the Synod of Bishops. In the postsynodal document *Pastores Gregis*, Blessed John Paul II writes,

> The ontological transformation brought about by episcopal consecration, as a configuration to Christ, demands a lifestyle that manifests a "being with him." Consequently, during the Synod sessions, emphasis was laid on pastoral charity as being the fruit of the character bestowed by the sacrament and of its particular grace. Charity, it was said, is in a sense the heart of the ministry of the Bishop, who is drawn into a dynamic pastoral *pro-existence* whereby he is impelled to live, like Christ the Good Shepherd, for the Father and for others, in the daily gift of self. (11)
>
> Here it is not only a matter of an *existentia* but indeed of a *pro-existentia*, that is to say, of a way of living inspired by the supreme model of Christ the Lord and which is spent totally in worship of the Father and in service of neighbor. (13)

What Blessed John Paul writes about the ministry of bishops is equally instructive for all priests. Our ministry is *for others* precisely because we have been made and ordained *for the worship of God.* By saying yes to the cross, not only do we give ourselves to God—for with Jesus, from the cross, we priests are also *given* by the Father to those he loves. Having *given ourselves to him,* and *having been given by him* to shepherd those he loves, we belong to all, and they to us.

Priestly celibacy is a sign that in and with Jesus *we are given* by the Father in a definitive way to those he loves, his family, to shepherd and father them. Priestly celibacy is a sign of our *pro existentia,* our being for God and, through him, for *every other.* Pope Benedict has reiterated that this is why priestly celibacy is not only *spousal;* it is also *Eucharistic.* The Words of Institution in the priest's daily celebration of the Eucharist form the agenda and orientation of each day—of each moment of his day.

⊞ ⊞ ⊞

Returning to the home of the beloved disciple and Mary, we see the embodiment of the Church herself and the atmosphere in which priests are called to live and minister. Moved and changed by the intimate friendship of prayer, we become signs of contradiction, and therefore signs of hope, with Jesus. At the same time, with Jesus and Mary, we are stretched on the cross and learn to give ourselves. Jesus tells us who our family is (*There is your son! There is your mother!*). He tells us for whom we are *father,* and our fathering bears fruit beyond our imagining. We are men *given,* and thus the Eucharist is the center of our lives. Our lives bespeak our deepest reality: "We are *for you,* because we are *in him.*"

I end with a beautiful poem by Charlotte Barr titled, simply, "John."

> beloved one
> more than a young girl's
> was the surge
> of your white love
> for the young messiah

when virgins embrace
the union is not flesh
it is fire
and the seed endures.

all the fierce young eagles
remember a time
when friends
could be lovers
when mass was unsaid
and the word unwritten
and jesus sat
holding the giddy head.[7]

8

A Recent Study of Celibacy and the Priesthood: What Do the Data Tell Us?

Rev. Msgr. Stephen J. Rossetti, PhD, DMin

When it comes to celibacy, there are many assumptions, projections, strong feelings, and exaggerations. Reflections on celibacy range from exalted tributes to dark condemnations; images evoked range from angelic portrayals to innuendoes of institutional deviancy. Like many issues in our increasingly bifurcated society, the gulf is growing between those who praise and those who condemn. Today, the window for dialogue or reconciliation is closing.

Perhaps a way forward is to begin a dialogue based upon on demonstrable facts, so valued in our scientific age, and on the lived experience of those who commit themselves to priestly celibacy. Surely the strongest argument, for or against, is what actually happens to those who spend decades engaged in this celibate living.

As one who teaches theology to seminarians, I often say to them, "Never be afraid of the truth." Truth fashioned our created world. Whenever and wherever truth is discovered, it is a reflection of the one Truth. More concretely, if celibacy results in the denigration of the human person, then such a life cannot be from God. But if celibacy, when lived with integrity and generosity, results in a flowering of one's personhood, then God's life-giving grace must be at work.

So, what is the experience of our priests who have committed themselves to celibate living? What is the truth? This is the question investigated in this chapter.

To examine the experience of our priests, I conducted two large surveys. The first was accomplished in 2004 and included 1,242 priests; the second was done in 2009 with 2,482 priests.

In the 2004 study, priests of sixteen dioceses around the United States were given a written survey. They came from a broad range of dioceses from every section of the country. These included all sizes of dioceses from smaller rural ones to those in large urban cities. Surveys were either handed out at diocesan priest convocations (nine dioceses) or directly mailed to all priests (seven dioceses). A substantial 64.9 percent of the priests responded, which is a good response rate.

For the 2009 survey, twenty-three dioceses mailed out the survey to all their priests. Again, there was a good response rate; this time it was 57 percent. It included 2,145 diocesan priests and 337 religious priests serving in these dioceses.

Both surveys were anonymous and confidential. While this was not a random survey, the broad range of dioceses across the country plus the good response rates suggest that the information collected is likely to be largely representative of the priests of the United States.

The data were analyzed using the PASW 18 software (Predictive Analytics SoftWare, SPSS).

PRIESTLY HAPPINESS

First, the study investigated priestly happiness.[1] As a group, are these celibate priests happy or unhappy? It is especially helpful if we can compare them to their lay counterparts.

When the self-reported rates of priestly happiness were computed, the results were very high and thus very positive (see table 1). In the 2004 survey, 90 percent agreed or strongly agreed that they were happy as priests; in the 2009 survey, 92.4 percent agreed or strongly agreed that they were happy.

After years of reading scandalous media accounts of the problems in priesthood, such results were unexpected by many. As a group, how can priests report high levels of happiness in the midst of such painful times? As the *Hartford Courant* reported in 2003, "In the wake of one scandal after another, the image of the genial, saintly cleric has given way to that of a lonely, dispirited figure living an unhealthy life that breeds sexual deviations."[2]

The best confirmation of a research study is similar findings in another study done by different researchers using a different sample. In fact, this has been done several times measuring priestly happiness, and each time there are similar findings: priests report about a 90 percent rate of satisfaction with their lives and priesthood.

For example, a 2001 National Federation of Priest Councils (NFPC) survey of 1,279 priests found that 94 percent reported being "happy" or "very happy." A 2001 CARA poll of 1,234 priests found that 88 percent "strongly agree" and 11 percent "somewhat agree" with the statement "Overall, I am satisfied with my life as a priest." Similarly, a 2003 informal study by the *Hartford Courant* of 107 priests also found that 94 percent of

Table 1. "Overall, I am happy as a priest"

	Strongly agree (%)	Agree (%)	Unsure/ Neutral (%)	Disagree (%)	Strongly disagree (%)
2004 survey	39.2	50.8	5.2	4.5	0.3
2009 survey	42.5	49.9	5.0	2.1	0.5

priests agree that "most of the time, I am happy with my life as a priest." Another informal study of 1,854 priests by the *Los Angeles Times* in 2002 reported that 91 percent were satisfied with the "way your life as a priest is going these days."[3]

All of these recent surveys of priestly happiness, accomplished by a variety of different researchers using different methods and different samples, have come to the same findings: about 90 percent of priests say they are happy as priests. How does this compare to the laity? The answer is clear: very favorably. Comparing the NFPC results to a 1972–1974 National Opinion Research Center (NORC) study of 32,029 Americans found that priests were consistently much happier than laity of all age groups.[4] Likewise, NORC's 2006 General Social Survey of twenty-seven thousand Americans found that clergy (Protestant and Catholic) had the highest rates of job satisfaction (87 percent very satisfied) of any job holders in the United States as well as the highest rates of personal happiness.[5] Not only are Catholic clergy reporting exceptionally high levels of personal happiness, but also they are reporting the highest of any professionals or job holders across the nation.

PRIESTHOOD AND LONELINESS

A common conception is that, because priests are celibate, they must be lonely. In my 2004 study, I gave the priests the statement "I suffer from loneliness." In the survey results, 3.5 percent strongly agreed, 18.7 percent agreed, 16.1 percent were neutral, 42.5 percent disagreed, and 19.2 percent strongly disagreed. Thus, 22.2 percent of priests agreed or strongly agreed that they suffer from loneliness.

It is difficult to compare these results to loneliness studies of the laity because the methods used and the results across many different studies are so disparate. However, a look at some loneliness studies suggests that priestly loneliness rates appear to be comparable to their lay peers if not lower. For example, a 2010 AARP survey of Americans forty-five years old or older found that 35 percent would be classified as lonely.

When never-married respondents were tallied, arguably more similar to celibate priests, the number jumped to 51 percent.[6]

In a striking study by Miller McPherson, Lynn Smith-Lovin, and Matthew E. Brashears, there was a marked decrease in Americans having someone to talk to about "important matters" in their lives. The modal number of such close friendships was three in 1984 but dropped to zero in 2004. People having no one to discuss important matters with increased from 10 percent to 25 percent during the same time frame. These and other statistics have suggested that social isolation among Americans is increasing.[7]

In my 2009 survey, however, priests reported a strong network of friends, both lay and priest friends. In response to the statement "I share my problems and feelings with close friends," 83.2 percent of priests either agreed or strongly agreed. In the same survey, 87.6 percent strongly agreed or agreed that "I currently have close priests friends," and 93 percent agreed or strongly agreed that "I have good lay friends who are an emotional support for me personally."

As isolation and loneliness among Americans in general appears to be on the rise, the great majority of celibate priests report strong personal connections with the laity and with other priests.

CELIBACY AND LONELINESS

I then narrowed in more closely on the following question: is difficulty with celibacy correlated to priestly loneliness? Using PASW 18 software with the 2009 survey numbers, I correlated a number of variables with loneliness to determine which ones were most strongly correlated and thus predictive of priestly loneliness. Table 2 reports five of the most important predictors of loneliness.[8]

The variable View of Celibacy was composed of two items that were combined: "Despite its challenges, celibacy has been a grace for me personally" and "I believe God has called me to live a celibate life." These were combined based upon factor analyses and subsequent Cronbach's alpha. Thus, the two items were statistically shown to comprise a single larger variable that I have called View of Celibacy. Since the correlation of this variable with loneliness was −0.33, as priests were less likely to see celibacy as a grace and a divine calling, they were more likely to be lonely.

However, it is very interesting that there were four other variables that were as strongly predictive of loneliness as celibacy, if not a slight bit stronger. In table 2, these are listed as Anger Problems, Sexual Conflicts, Childhood Mental Problems, and Dysfunctional Childhood.[9] These survey items indicate the presence of emotional and psychological problems in the priest's background. Thus, while problems with celibacy can be predictive of loneliness, there are psychological problems that are equally predictive if not more so. Priests who come from dysfunctional backgrounds and also have anger and sexual problems are much more likely to suffer from loneliness than those who do not.

Is loneliness a function of celibacy? These data suggest that priests do not have a unique problem with loneliness and might even be better off than other people. Certainly, a positive adjustment to celibacy will likely be a significant deterrent to loneliness and a priest who struggles with celibacy is more likely to be lonely. However, other factors are equally, if not more, important in predicting loneliness, including the presence of personal psychological deficits and internal conflicts.

If a priest suffers from loneliness, he should hesitate in presuming that marriage would solve his problem. The source of his loneliness could easily be in his own difficulty in connecting

Table 2. 2009 survey: Correlations with the survey item: "I suffer from loneliness"

Variable	Pearson's r
Anger Problems	.35
Sexual Conflicts	.35
Childhood Mental Problems	.34
Dysfunctional Childhood	.33
View of Celibacy	-.33

with others and his inner psychological deficits. Whether one is a priest or a layperson, loneliness is sometimes part of the fallen human condition. Finding inner healing for one's personal deficits and developing a network of friends with whom one can share one's joys and struggles are likely to be critical factors in overcoming loneliness.

PRIESTLY HAPPINESS AND CELIBACY

Given that priests reported such a strong sense of personal happiness, all the variables in the 2009 survey were correlated with happiness to see which ones were most likely to influence priestly happiness. The results in table 3 list the top ten variables. These are the most important factors that surfaced in this study to predict what makes a happy priest.

The most important variable predicting priestly happiness was the presence of Inner Peace. This variable was composed of two survey items: "I feel a sense of inner peace" and "I have a good self-image." Not surprising, those who have a sense of inner peace are much more likely to be happy priests. People tend to be happy in whatever lifestyle or vocation they are in if they are content inside. An unhappy priest is likely to be an unhappy married person and vice versa. Inner peace is

Table 3. 2009 survey: Correlations with Priestly Happiness

Variable	Pearson's *r*
Inner Peace	.59
Relationship to God	.53
View of Celibacy	.47
Lonely and Unappreciated	-.46
Relationship to the Bishop	.38
Anger Problems	-.38
Dysfunctional Childhood	-.37
Obedience to Religious Authority	.36
Close Friends	.35
Childhood Mental Health Problems	-.35

something we bring to our jobs or vocations, and if we have it, regardless of where we find ourselves, we are more likely to be happy. So, I recommend the following to priests who are unhappy: if you want to become a happier person, before you start changing your environment or vocation, first look inside.

The second-strongest variable predicting priestly happiness was Relationship to God, which included five questions about his relationship to God such as having a nourishing relationship to God, feeling a sense of closeness to God, and feeling that God loves him personally.[10] It was surprising that a statistical survey could demonstrate so strongly the critical nature of a priest's spiritual life for his well-being and happiness. The statistical output was clear: the strength of a priest's relationship to God is of the greatest importance to his priestly and personal well-being. Moreover, the strongest predictor of the previous variable, Inner Peace, was also Relationship to God, thus increasing the importance of the latter variable even more (Pearson's $r = 0.55$).

Finally, the third-strongest correlation and thus predictor of priestly happiness was the variable View of Celibacy. In the wake of the findings in this study, I have begun to emphasize to priest gatherings the great importance of priests coming to a deeper appreciation of their celibate commitment. Greater than a number of other psychological and personal variables in the study, a priest's integration of his promise of celibacy will be a very large predictor of how happy he will be as a priest (Pearson's $r = 0.47$).

CELIBACY AS CALLING AND GRACE

These research results suggest that a priest needs to move beyond a mere acceptance of celibacy: he needs to integrate it as a calling from God and as a personal grace. These were the two constitutive elements of the following variables: "Despite its challenges, celibacy has been a grace for me personally" and "I believe God has called me to live a celibate life." The priest who is stuck at the level of viewing celibacy only as a discipline imposed by the Church is much less likely to be a happy priest.

Experiencing celibacy as a divine calling and a grace implies that the priest's integration of celibacy has reached a deep internalization and thus his spiritual life has reached a profound level. It means that the priest has come to experience a direct and personal calling from God. Moreover, it suggests he has experienced himself as personally blessed and graced by God. This is a direct connection with God that must necessarily bode well for his well-being and happiness.

Moreover, a strong and deep integration of one's celibate commitment is not easy and challenges the priest in a number of personal and spiritual ways. He must be accepting of the Church's celibate tradition and thus its leadership, submitting himself in service to the Church and to others. To live celibacy well, he must also have strong relational skills. He must be able to relate well as a chaste celibate to the laity and to his brother priests. He must develop strong pastoral skills so that his pastoral ministry will be fruitful and nurturing for others and for himself. He must learn to connect with God in a regular and intimate way. Adding up all of these essential priestly values, one can say that a deep integration of celibacy requires a profound priestly spirituality, and thus it is no wonder celibacy is a constitutive element of priestly happiness.

What percentage of our priests have reportedly reached this deep priestly spirituality? These results, using the 2009 study, are in table 4.

It is edifying and encouraging that 78.2 percent of priests either strongly agree or agree that "I believe God has called me to live a celibate life" and that 75.1 percent strongly agree or

Table 4. 2009 survey: View of Celibacy

	Strongly agree (%)	Agree (%)	Neutral (%)	Disagree (%)	Strongly disagree (%)
"I believe God has called me to live a celibate life"	33.2	45.0	13.6	6.1	2.1
"Despite its challenges, celibacy has been a grace for me personally"	22.8	52.3	13.0	8.4	3.4

agree that, "despite its challenges, celibacy has been a grace for me personally." The numbers indicate that three-quarters of priests have integrated their promise of celibacy in a profound way. Given the critical importance of this variable for priestly happiness, this helps to explain why priestly rates of happiness are so high.

However, these numbers also indicate that about one-quarter of priests have *not* reached such a positive experience of their celibate promise. This is not an insignificant number and suggests the need for additional formation and ongoing formation in celibacy.

RELIGIOUS OBEDIENCE AND VIEW OF CELIBACY

Since a priest's View of Celibacy is so important, the next step is to investigate statistically the most important variables contributing to this positive view of celibacy. What helps a priest to arrive at this integration? These are presented in table 5 from the 2009 study. Some of the variables that surfaced as strong contributors might be, at first glance, somewhat surprising.

There are two types of variables in table 5: spiritual and psychological. The spiritual values contributed most strongly. They are the first four variables. The last five are more psychological variables. Once again it is interesting and important that

Table 5. 2009 survey: Correlations with View of Celibacy

Variable	Pearson's *r*
Obedience to Religious Authority	.49
Prayer and Sacrament of Penance	.47
Devotion to Mary	.47
Relationship to God	.36
Lonely and Unappreciated	-.31
Sexual Conflicts	-.28
Dysfunctional Childhood	-.24
Anger Problems	-.21
Childhood Mental Problems	-.20

the spiritual values were more highly predictive of one's View of Celibacy and thus of greater significance in priestly well-being. However, the psychological issues were significant and cannot be ignored.

The variable that was first and thus the first predictor of a priest's View of Celibacy was the single survey item "Obedience to religious authority is an important value for me." This was another surprise for this researcher: why should this one survey item be so strongly correlated to a priest's View of Celibacy ($r = 0.49$)? What does religious obedience have to do with living celibacy well?

The relationship between the two would be good fodder for discussion at a priestly gathering. Some initial thoughts surface. First, valuing obedience to religious authority suggests an attitude of humble and self-giving service. The priest who is obedient to his religious superiors and who lives the rigors of chaste celibacy is willing and able to deny himself in the service of others and the Church. He offers himself for the spiritual welfare of others.

On the other hand, this study showed that a narcissistic self-entitlement was detrimental to one's View of Celibacy ($r = -0.15$), hence the negative correlation. Moreover, narcissistic traits are more likely to be associated with feelings of loneliness and not being appreciated ($r = 0.29$) as well as having anger problems ($r = 0.28$).[11]

It has long been said that a priest's celibate life is a gift of himself to the people and to the Church. Priesthood itself, if lived well, is not primarily for the priest's own benefit; although certainly a profound grace for him, priesthood is foremost for the good of others. If a man comes into priesthood with the attitude that this sacrament is about him or primarily focused on his own well-being, he is missing the essential element of humble service. As is true of Christianity as a whole, when the priest gives of himself, he paradoxically finds himself. When he serves the needs of others, he finds true happiness and inner peace.

OTHER VARIABLES CONTRIBUTING
TO VIEW OF CELIBACY

Table 5 indicated several other important variables predictive of a priest's View of Celibacy. Second in importance was the amount of time the priest spent in prayer, including praying the Liturgy of the Hours, and how often he received the Sacrament of Penance.[12] The more time he spent in prayer, being faithful to the Liturgy of the Hours, and regular confession himself, the more likely he was to have a positive View of Celibacy ($r = 0.47$).

This strong correlation is easy to grasp. As one prays more and engages directly in spiritual practices, one would expect a priest to be open to God's grace. Similarly, Relationship to God was also strongly predictive of a positive View of Celibacy ($r = 0.36$). Prayer and developing a relationship to God are critical in integrating celibacy. Celibacy lived well is more about a "yes" than a "no." It is a "yes" to a different way of loving. It is a direct, self-giving love of God and love of God's people.

Also, it is interesting to note that the three promises a priest makes at his diaconate and priestly ordinations are all present here: celibacy, Liturgy of the Hours, and obedience. It suggests that, as a priest lives priesthood with integrity, fulfilling the public promises that he made, he is more likely to be happy and to find a deep meaning to his life.

Another spiritual variable that surfaced was a priest's Devotion to Mary, comprised of two survey items: "I have a devotion to the Virgin Mary" and "Mary is an important part of my priestly life." The correlation between this variable and View of Celibacy was also a strong $r = 0.47$. Clearly, there is a strong connection between a priest's integration of celibacy and his personal devotion to the Mother of God.

While Jesus on the cross gave Mary to all people, "Behold your mother," it was no accident that the person representing humankind was an apostle. While Mary is the mother of all, she is particularly close to her priests. Priests are uniquely configured to Christ and thus, when she looks upon the faces of her priests, she sees the beloved face of her son, Jesus. And priests have traditionally had a special devotion to this holiest of women. For many, she becomes the woman in their lives. Could one have a better female presence while walking through the travails of life?

The final five variables contributing to a priest's View of Celibacy were psychological variables: Lonely and Unappreciated, Sexual Conflicts, Dysfunctional Childhood, Anger Problems, and Childhood Mental Problems. Their correlations ranged from $r = -0.31$ to $r = -0.20$. The negative correlations indicate an inverse relationship. As these psychological problems increase, one's ability to live a chaste celibacy with happiness and peace decreases. The Church should never underestimate the difficulties of living a celibate priesthood with integrity for those with psychological deficits. There are clear indications that there was a time in the Church, a few decades ago, when this was the case, and many are still paying the price. While spiritual values are the strongest predictors of a priesthood well lived, the psychological variables are significant and not far behind in importance.

In summary, the data suggest that a priest with a deep integration of his celibate commitment is likely to be someone who is an obedient son of the Church and has a self-giving love of his people. He is more likely to have a personal devotion to Mary and a nourishing relationship to God. He is likely to say Liturgy of the Hours faithfully, go to confession regularly, and pray privately for a significant amount of time each day. Moreover, he probably has good lay and priest friends, and is unlikely to be burdened by serious psychological problems or inner conflicts. Such a man will profess to be happy as a priest and sees celibacy, despite its challenges, as a calling from God and a personal grace.

ORDINATION COHORTS AND MANDATORY CELIBACY

One of the interesting research findings that surfaced was the difference between ordination cohorts. There were marked differences on how younger, older, and middle-aged priests viewed mandatory celibacy.

In the 2004 survey, priests were given the statement "I support the requirement that priests live a celibate life." In table 6, we see the very large differences. For priests ordained thirty to thirty-nine years, only 37.9 percent either agreed or strongly agreed with mandatory celibacy. But for priests ordained less than ten years, the number more than doubled to 81.4 percent. This is an enormous difference.

Table 6. 2004 survey: Numerical count for years ordained and "I support the requirement that priests live a celibate life"

	"I support the requirement that priests live a celibate life"					
	Strongly agree	Agree	Unsure	Disagree	Strongly disagree	Total
Number of years as a priest						
1–9						
Count	96	66	17	13	7	199
%	48.2	33.2	8.5	6.5	3.5	100.0
10–19						
Count	70	55	24	41	25	215
%	32.6	25.6	11.2	19.1	11.6	100.0
20–29						
Count	51	67	47	53	43	261
%	19.5	25.7	18.0	20.3	16.5	100.0
30–39						
Count	50	56	34	80	60	280
%	17.9	20.0	12.1	28.6	21.4	100.0
40–49						
Count	49	44	25	47	33	198
%	24.7	22.2	12.6	23.7	16.7	100.0
50 years and above						
Count	23	24	9	12	9	77
%	29.9	31.2	11.7	15.6	11.7	100.0
Total						
Count	339	312	156	246	177	1230
%	27.6	25.4	12.7	20.0	14.4	100.0

If these trends continue, support for mandatory celibacy among priests in the United States will increase as more of these young men are ordained and enter the priesthood, while more of the older priests retire. Ironically, as support for celibacy decreases in secular society, the support among priests is rising sharply. The celibate priest who is strong in this commitment will increasingly become a sign of contradiction for the secular world around him.

This difference between ordination cohorts is not surprising when one considers the self-identified differences in their theological stance. Each of the respondents was given the statement "Theologically, I am considered to be" with the possible responses being very liberal, liberal, middle of the road, conservative, or very conservative. The newly ordained priests (less than ten years) self-identified as being much more conservative than the priests in their middle years (thirty to thirty-nine years). For those ordained less than ten years, 45.2 percent identified themselves as conservative/very conservative while only 6.1 percent identified themselves as liberal/very liberal. On the other hand, for those ordained thirty to thirty-nine years, it was reversed. A larger 33 percent identified themselves as liberal/very liberal, whereas only 13.6 percent identified themselves as conservative/very conservative.

There is a clear shift in theological orientation between priests in their middle years and younger priests as found in this 2004 survey. This shift strongly affects their support for mandatory celibacy as seen in the following figure (see figure 1).

The differences between liberal and conservatives priests in their support for mandatory celibacy were stunning. Essentially, priests who identified as conservative (83.4 percent) or very conservative (92.6 percent) were strongly in favor of mandatory celibacy. Whereas, priests who identified as liberal (71 percent) or very liberal (100 percent) were strongly against mandatory celibacy. Given the almost black-and-white difference, one might say that support or nonsupport for mandatory celibacy is one of the defining characteristics for priests when they identify their theological stance. If they are against mandatory celibacy,

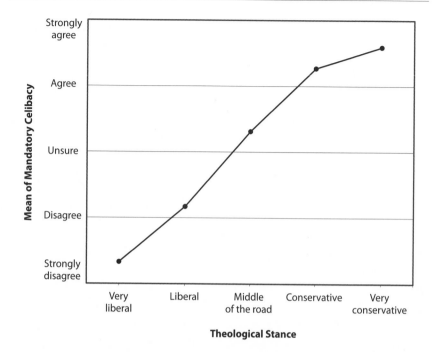

Figure 1: Support for mandatory celibacy by theological stance

they are, almost by definition, theologically liberal, and if they are in favor of mandatory celibacy, they are, almost by definition, theologically conservative, with few exceptions.

Given that a higher percentage of young priests identify themselves as theologically conservative, it is no surprise that support for mandatory celibacy is much higher among the younger priests. If the trend toward younger priests being more theologically conservative continues, then support for mandatory celibacy is likely to rise sharply in the years ahead. If this trend does continue, mandatory celibacy will disappear among Catholic priests in the United States as a "hot button" issue. I already see signs of the waning of this issue among priests.

WOULD PRIESTS MARRY?

The 2004 survey also gave the priests the statement "If priests were allowed to marry, I would get married." The overall percentage who agreed or strongly agreed was only 17.8

percent. It is fair to conclude that, even if mandatory celibacy were abolished, a small percentage would marry. Contrary to popular opinion, the large majority of priests are not feeling constrained by mandatory celibacy and are not "champing at the bit" to get married.

Given the sharp differences noted above between older and younger priests in their support for mandatory celibacy, one might expect the same sharp differences among these ordination cohorts in their desire to marry. However, the statistics indicated otherwise.

In fact, the differences between age cohorts were not large. Of the priests ordained less than ten years, 16.1 percent agreed or strongly agreed they would marry if given the chance. The percentage was 20.6 for those ordained ten to nineteen years and back to 16 percent for those ordained twenty to twenty-nine years. Only 20.6 percent of the group ordained thirty to thirty-nine years, the very group whose support for mandatory celibacy was so low, indicated they would marry if allowed.

Thus, there was a limited difference among age cohorts in a personal desire to marry, although a large difference in their support for mandatory celibacy. As noted above, the priests who were against mandatory celibacy identified themselves as liberal, and conversely, those who were in favor of mandatory celibacy identified themselves as conservative. Thus, the real issue of support for mandatory celibacy among priests appears to be less a personal desire to marry and more of a theological stance. Those who are against mandatory celibacy are so largely because they are against the idea in general as part of their theological vision. Those who are for mandatory celibacy are so largely because they are in favor of it as part of their different theological vision. But if given the chance to marry, both groups profess a desire to marry at about the same rather low percentage, 16 to 20 percent.

CONCLUDING COMMENTS

Perhaps one of the first conclusions to draw from these findings is the centrality of the commitment to celibacy in the life of a priest. It is one of the strongest predictors of priestly happiness. A priest who struggles throughout his priesthood with celibacy and sees it as a burden is unlikely to be a happy priest.

Happily, most priests, about three-quarters of them, view celibacy not as a burden but as a vocation and a grace, despite its challenges. This is good news indeed. And it should serve as a source of edification. To view one's celibacy as a calling and as a grace necessitates a profound spiritual life and a deep integration of this challenging commitment. It is inspiring that so many of our priests have done so.

Nevertheless, one-quarter of our priests have not yet reached such an integration. Priesthood today in our secular society poses many challenges. But for a man who struggles with his celibate commitment in the midst of a sex-crazed society, it must, at times, be excruciating. These men need additional support. In addition, the critical importance of living one's celibate life with integrity and grace necessitates that priestly formation and ongoing formation emphasize it with some regularity.

Such formation programs ought to include frank conversations among priests and among seminarians about the supports and the challenges for celibacy today. Reading spiritual texts that provide a solid theological framework are a necessary backdrop. At some point, the discussion ought to move to the concrete and the experiential. How is celibacy experienced today? What are some of the necessary supports for a celibate priest, and how can he mobilize such supports? Also, a frank discussion of what celibate living is like in our secular society, which treats sex as a commodity and with societal loneliness on the rise, should assist in making the discussion more concretely helpful.

The stakes are high. As we continue to read in the media, a priest who cannot live a celibate life with integrity is at risk for harmful behavior that may find its way into the public forum. The gulf between the witness of a celibate priest and a secular society addicted to sexual stimulation is widening. The new cohort of younger priests has the challenge and the calling to be such a witness. They are taking up this challenge with faith and fervor. Like all generations of frail human beings, there will be more than a few failures. But there will be many successes, and they will be a sign to the world that there is something more to the human person than what our materialistic society can see and touch.

In the beginning of this chapter, we explored the experience of our celibate priests and the truth that emerged. Clearly, celibacy for the sake of the kingdom does not cause one to become lonely and unhappy. In fact, priests are consistently shown to be much happier and more fulfilled than their lay counterparts. They have good friends, possess a strong spiritual life, and find their lives full of meaning. Instead of viewing their promise of celibacy as a burden, the strong majority sees it as a divine calling and a grace. Instead of making them miserable, celibacy is part of a larger calling that sets the priest apart as one uniquely chosen and blessed by God.

Each one of these priests is a living truth witnessing to a greater Truth. Each one is a challenge to a materialistic, secular society that has forgotten a dimension it cannot see yet should never have lost. The people asked Jesus for a sign; they wanted a miracle. In front of you now are such miracles, signs of contradiction, if you have the eyes to see and a heart that is open to the Truth.

Notes

1: Dimensions of Priestly Celibacy

1. *Perfectae caritatis* (Decree on the Up-to-Date Renewal of Religious Life), 12, in The Sixteen Basic Documents; *Vatican II: Constitutions, Decrees, Declarations*, ed. Austin Flannery (Northport, NY: Costello Publishing, 1996), 393.

2. Jean-Paul Sartre, *The Flies*, in *No Exit* and *The Flies*, trans. Stuart Gilbert, act 3 (New York: Knopf, 1954), 158–59.

3. St. Cyprian, *De habitu virginum (On Virginity)*, 22, trans. Angela Elizabeth Keenan (Washington, DC: Catholic University of America Press, 1932), 67.

4. St Augustine of Hippo, *The Confessions of St. Augustine*, book 10, 29, trans. John K. Ryan (Garden City, NY: Image Books, 1960), 256.

5. Rabbi Simeon ben Azzai, *Genesis Rabbah* 34, 14a.

6. Anders Nygren, *Agape and Eros*, trans. Philip S. Watson (Chicago: University of Chicago Press, 1953).

7. I have responded to this last argument in one of the meditations addressed to the papal household during Lent 2011 (Raniero Cantalamessa, "The Two Faces of Love: Eros and Agape," March 25, 2011, http://www.cantalamessa.org/?p=1331&lang=en).

8. Benedict XVI, *Deus caritas est (God Is Love)*, 7, 8.

9. Nicholas Cabasilas, *The Life in Christ*, 2, 19, trans. Carmino J. deCatanzaro (Crestwood, NY: St. Vladimir's Seminary Press, 1974), 96.

10. St. Augustine, "Sermon 243," 2: "Tangit Christum, qui credit in Christum," in *Sermons (230–272B)*, trans. Edmund Hill, vol. 7, *The Works of Saint Augustine*, ed. John E. Rotelle (New Rochelle, NY: New City Press, 1993), 89.

11. John Climacus, *Scala Paradisi*, 15, 98.

12. See St. Thomas Aquinas, *Summa Theologica*, I-IIae, q. 108, a. 4.

13. See St. Cyril of Jerusalem, *Catechesis* 26, 12 (Oxford, UK: John Henry Parker, 1837), 208.

14. St. Ignatius of Antioch, "Letter to Polycarp," 5, 2, in *The Apostolic Fathers*, trans. Francis X. Glimm et al. (New York: Christian Heritage, 1947), 126.

15. St. Augustine, *Confessions*, 6, 11. 150.

16. Ibid., 10, 29; see John K. Ryan's translation: "Give what you command, and command what you will. You enjoin continence" (255).

17. See, for example, St. Gregory of Nyssa, *On Virginity*, 3–4, in *The Fathers of the Church*, trans. Virginia Woods Callahan, vol. 58 (Washington, DC: Catholic University of America Press, 1967), 12–27.

18. Henri-Dominique Lacordaire, quoted in David Rice, *Shattered Vows* (Belfast: Blackstaff Press, 1990), 137.

2: Friends of the Bridegroom

1. Early Church legislation on clerical continence was generally based on what might be called the cultic motive (the notion that sexual abstinence is necessary for effective mediatory prayer), whereas contemporary Church teaching cites

what might be called the evangelical motive (Jesus' and Paul's recommendation of celibacy for the sake of the kingdom).

2. Prominent among these are Christian Cochini, *Apostolic Origins of Priestly Celibacy*, trans. Nelly Marans (San Francisco: Ignatius, 1990); Alfons Maria Cardinal Stickler, *The Case for Clerical Celibacy: Its Historical Development and Theological Foundations*, trans. Brian Ferme (San Francisco: Ignatius, 1995); and Roman Cholij, *Clerical Celibacy in East and West* (Leominster, MA: Fowler Wright, 1988). Other works include helpful but limited studies of the biblical material: Stefan Heid, *Celibacy in the Early Church: The Beginnings of a Discipline of Obligatory Continence for Clerics in East and West*, trans. Michael J. Miller (San Francisco: Ignatius, 2000), 24–57; Thomas McGovern, *Priestly Celibacy Today* (Princeton, NJ: Scepter, 1998), 70–98; Jean Galot, *Theology of the Priesthood*, trans. Roger Balducelli (San Francisco: Ignatius, 1984), 232–39; and Gary Selin, "On the Christological, Ecclesiological, and Eschatological Dimensions of Priestly Celibacy in *Presbyterorum Ordinis, Sacerdotalis Caelibatus* and Subsequent Magisterial Documents" (PhD diss., Catholic University of America, 2011). Ignace de la Potterie's chapter on "The Biblical Foundations of Priestly Celibacy," in *For Love Alone: Reflections on Priestly Celibacy* (Maynooth, Ireland: St. Paul's, 1993), 13–30, limits itself to the three "*unius uxoris vir*" passages in the pastoral letters. The present chapter likewise does not claim to be exhaustive.

3. The gift of offspring is likewise the first blessing associated with obedience to the covenant (Dt 28:4, 11) and often celebrated in the prophetic literature and psalms (cf. Ps 127:3–5; 128:3; 144:12).

4. John Paul II, *Man and Woman He Created Them: A Theology of the Body*, trans. Michael Waldstein (Boston: Pauline, 2006), 417. Here and in all other quotations from John Paul II, emphasis is in the original.

5. Although Jeremiah was of priestly lineage (Jer 1:1), he apparently was unable to minister as a priest since he belonged to the ostracized family of Abiathar (1 Kgs 2:26). His celibacy was linked not to his priesthood but to his prophetic office.

6. *Jewish Study Bible* (Oxford: Oxford University Press, 2004), 958; cf. b. *Makkot* 23b.

7. b. *Kiddushin* 29b. b. *Yebamoth* 61b–64b.

8. b. *Yebamoth* 63a; cf. 62b; *Genesis Rabbah* 17 (11d). Rabbi Eliezer ben Hyrcanus is said to have equated a man's refusal to procreate with murder (b. *Yebamoth* 63a).

9. According to Josephus, the Essenes "do not absolutely deny the fitness of marriage, and the succession of mankind thereby continued; but they guard against the lascivious behavior of women, and are persuaded that none of them preserve their fidelity to one man" (*War of the Jews* 2.8.2; cf. *Antiquities* 18.1.5). See also Philo, *Hypothetica* (preserved in Eusebius, *Praeparatio Evangelica* 8.11.1–18); and Pliny the Elder, *Natural History* 5.18.73, 1Q7:5–7. See John Meier, *A Marginal Jew: Rethinking the Historical Jesus*, vol. 1 (New York: Doubleday, 1991), 332–45.

10. Philo, *On the Contemplative Life*.

11. b. *Yebamoth* 63b.

12. In Mark 7:14–23, Jesus indicates that the Mosaic dietary laws were a provisional dispensation whose purpose is now fulfilled in the purity of heart made possible by the new covenant. The early church gradually interpreted this

abrogation as extending to all the Mosaic ceremonial laws (cf., e.g., Acts 8:36; 10:1–48; 15:19–20; Gal 5:11).

13. b. *Sabbath* 87a. The rabbis find a confirmation of this conclusion in Deuteronomy 5:30–31, where God instructs the Israelites, "Return to your tents," that is, resume marital relations, but tells Moses, in contrast, "But you, stand here by me" (Dt 5:30–31).

14. It is important to note the distinction between ritual purity and moral purity, a distinction not yet explicit in the purity laws of Leviticus. A person could be rendered unclean not only by immoral behavior but also by various normal bodily processes or by diseases that have no bearing on moral conduct.

15. Cf. also 2 Samuel 11, which portrays Uriah the Hittite as virtuously observing the abstinence requirement for soldiers on active duty, in sharp contrast to David's lascivious behavior.

16. Gabriel's address to Mary, "Rejoice!" (Lk 1:28), is an echo of the invitation to Messianic joy addressed by the prophets to daughter Zion (cf. Zep 3:14–15; Zec 9:9; Jl 2:21–23), hinting that Mary is the embodiment of the new people of God, the Church.

17. Like the wilderness tabernacle that contained the ark, Mary is "overshadowed" by the divine glory (Lk 1:35; Ex 40:35); at her coming, there is a shout of joy and the infant John leaps in the womb of his mother, as David leaped and danced before the ark (Lk 1:41–42; 2 Sm 6:15–16); and her presence evokes an exclamation of humble awe from Elizabeth, like that of David before the ark (Lk 1:43; 2 Sm 6:9). For these and other parallels designed to typologically establish Mary as the new ark, see Scott Hahn, *Hail Holy Queen: The Mother of God in the Word of God* (New York: Doubleday, 2001), 64.

18. W. D. Davies and Dale C. Allison, *Matthew 19–28*, International Critical Commentary (London: T&T Clark, 2004), 24–25. In later rabbinic literature, "eunuch" was a term of derision for single men; cf. b. *Yebamoth* 80b.

19. Isaiah 56:3–5, however, prophesies the full acceptance of eunuchs in the temple of the Messianic era, a promise that Luke, in his account of the baptism of the Ethiopian eunuch (Acts 8:26–40), portrays as fulfilled in the Christian community.

20. Davies and Allison, *Matthew 19–28*, 25.

21. Although the term "eunuch" applies literally only to men, Jesus here uses it metaphorically, and his invitation to celibacy for the kingdom has always been understood as addressed to women as well as men.

22. John Paul II, *Man and Woman*, 423, 418.

23. Cf. Is 24:23; 52:7; Zep 3:14–15; Zec 14:9.

24. See Raniero Cantalamessa, *Virginity: A Positive Approach to Celibacy for the Sake of the Kingdom of Heaven*, trans. Charles Serignat (New York: Alba House, 1995), 6–7.

25. Christopher West, "Celibacy for the Kingdom and the Fulfillment of Human Sexuality," accessed January 24, 2012, http://www.christopherwest.com/.

26. John Paul II, *Man and Woman*, 393.

27. Ibid., 395.

28. Ibid., 393.

29. Cf. Is 54:5–8; 62:4–5; Jer 2:1–3; Ez 16; Hos 2:2, 14–20.

30. John Paul II, *Man and Woman*, 488.

31. In the Old Testament, new wine (or sweet wine) is an image of the joy and abundant blessings that God would bestow on his people in the Messianic age (Jl 3:18; Am 9:13–14; Zec 9:16–17).

32. See Ignace de la Potterie, *Mary in the Mystery of the Covenant*, trans. Bertrand Buby (New York: Alba House, 1992), 157–208.

33. Other clues in the text include the presence of "the mother of Jesus" only at Cana and the cross; her title "woman" in both scenes, hinting at the fulfillment of Genesis 3:15; the presence of wine; and the references to the Passover (Jn 2:13), the "hour" of Jesus' passion (Jn 2:4), and the manifestation of his "glory" (Jn 2:11). The Cana episode thus symbolically anticipates Christ's passion, revealing it as a nuptial mystery.

34. McGovern, *Priestly Celibacy Today*, 79.

35. See John Paul II, *Man and Woman*, 434.

36. John Paul II, *Man and Woman*, 437.

37. This was the traditional role of the "friend of the bridegroom" or best man—a role that rabbinic tradition assigned to Moses in the marriage of God and Israel. See Raymond Brown, *The Gospel According to John (i–xii)*, Anchor Bible (Garden City, NY: Doubleday, 1966), 152.

38. McGovern, *Priestly Celibacy Today*, 82.

39. Paul's allowance of temporary abstinence for married couples, "that you may devote yourselves to prayer" (1 Cor 7:5), has sometimes been misinterpreted as implying a cultic motive for continence, that is, the idea that the marital act is incompatible with effective mediatory prayer (cf. Cochini, *Apostolic Origins*, 435). But there are no grounds for this interpretation in the text. Paul counsels abstinence not for the sake of effective prayer but for undivided devotion to prayer—literally, "that you may have leisure [*scholasēte*] for prayer." Elsewhere he exhorts all Christians without exception to "pray constantly" (1 Thes 5:17; cf. Eph 6:18; Rom 12:12; Col 4:2), and often mentions the effectiveness of their prayer (Rom 15:30; 2 Cor 1:11; Phil 1:19; Col 4:3; Phlm 1:22).

40. George Montague, *First Corinthians*, Catholic Commentary on Sacred Scripture (Grand Rapids, MI: Baker Academic, 2011), 135.

41. Maximos Davies, a Byzantine Catholic monk, makes this point forcefully in "Celibacy in Context," *First Things* 128 (December 2002): 13–15.

42. Ibid.

43. Will Deming, for an example, proposes such an interpretation in *Paul on Marriage and Celibacy: The Hellenistic Background of 1 Corinthians 7* (Cambridge: Cambridge University Press, 1995).

44. McGovern, *Priestly Celibacy Today*, 83; cf. John Paul II, *Man and Woman*, 448–49.

45. It is possible, though by no means certain, that the giving up of "children" (in all three Synoptic accounts; cf. Mk 10:29; Mt 19:29) is intended to imply the giving up of marital relations, that is, the possibility of future children.

46. Jesus is identified as "priest" and "high priest" of the new covenant only by the writer to the Hebrews, who was probably expressing an original insight but one rooted in ideas already germinating in the New Testament period.

47. For a summary of these see Brant Pitre, "Jesus, the New Temple, and the New Priesthood," *Letter and Spirit* 4 (2008): 47–83. See also Crispin H. T.

Fletcher-Louis, "Jesus as the High Priestly Messiah," parts 1 and 2, *Journal for the Study of the Historical Jesus* 4, no. 2 (2006): 155–75 and 5, no. 1 (2007): 57–79; and André Feuillet, *The Priesthood of Christ and His Ministers*, trans. Matthew J. O'Connell (Garden City, NY: Doubleday, 1975).

48. Thomas Lane, "The Ministerial Priesthood in the New Testament," *Incarnate Word* 2 (2009): 723–40.

49. Ibid., 726.

50. Fletcher-Louis, "Jesus as the High Priestly Messiah," 2:76.

51. Albert Cardinal Vanhoye, *Old Testament Priests and the New Priest According to the New Testament*, trans. J. B. Orchard, rev. ed. (Leominster, MA: Gracewing, 2009), 268.

52. Ibid., 267–69.

53. Cf. Nm 18:8–19; Dt 18:3, which detail how the Israelite priests are to be compensated for their ministry.

54. Cf. Vanhoye, *Old Testament Priests*, 270–72.

55. Hence most modern English translations use the expression "believing wife" (ESV, NIV, NRSV) or "Christian wife" (NAB, NJB). See John Granger Cook, "1 Cor 9,5: The Women of the Apostles," *Biblica* 89 (2008): 352–68; and Gordon Fee, *The First Epistle to the Corinthians*, NICNT (Grand Rapids, MI: Eerdmans, 1987), 403.

56. Tertullian, *De Monogamia* 8; Jerome, *Adversus Jovinianum* 1.26; Augustine, *De opera monachorum* 5.

57. Several Western manuscripts (F G a b Tert Ambst Pel) have the plural *gynaikas* and omit "sister." But it is highly unlikely that this is the original reading. See Fee, *First Epistle to the Corinthians*, 397n1.

58. See Clement of Alexandria, *Stromata* 3.53.5. The Council of Girona (AD 517) stipulated that "if [clerics] have been married before their ordinations, they should not live with their wives—the latter being now sisters to them—if they have no access to brothers to serve as their witness [to continence]." Canon 6, quoted in Cochini, *Apostolic Origins*, 326. Gregory the Great writes approvingly of a priest who "after he had taken orders . . . still loved his wife as his sister" (*Dialogues* 4.11).

59. Cochini, *Apostolic Origins*, 7. However, it should be noted that such a discipline would be in tension with Paul's realism regarding the difficulty of sexual self-restraint in 1 Cor 7:8–9. Also, the fact that Eastern Christianity since at least the Council of Trullo (AD 691) equally claimed apostolic authority for permitting marital intercourse for priests and deacons suggests that such a standard was not regarded as universally binding on ordained ministers in the primitive Church. See the critiques of Cochini's thesis by Adrian Hastings, "The Origins of Priestly Celibacy," *Heythrop Journal* 24 (1983): 171–77; and Roger Balducelli, "The Apostolic Origins of Clerical Continence: A Critical Appraisal of a New Book," *Theological Studies* 43 (1982): 693–705.

60. This interpretation coheres with the use of "sister" in 1 Timothy 5:1–2 regarding chaste relationships within the Christian community: "Treat . . . older women like mothers, younger women like sisters, in all purity."

61. Clement of Alexandria, *Stromata* 3.53.3. Translation from Gerald Lewis Bray, ed., *1–2 Corinthians*, Ancient Christian Commentary on Scripture (Downers Grove, IL: InterVarsity, 1999), 80.

62. For the purposes of this chapter, there is no need to take a position on the authenticity of the pastoral letters. For arguments in favor of Pauline authorship, see George Montague, *First and Second Timothy, Titus*, Catholic Commentary on Sacred Scripture (Grand Rapids, MI: Baker Academic, 2008), 16–24.

63. Although some interpret "husband of one wife" as excluding polygamy rather than remarriage after widowhood, this is unlikely since monogamy was a basic expectation for all Christians, but the formula is used only for ordained ministers and enrolled widows. Moreover, the corresponding stipulation for widows, that they be "wife of one husband," clearly refers to remarriage after widowhood since polyandry was not practiced.

64. See, for instance, Pope Siricius, *Cum in unum* decretal; Synod of Rome (AD 386); and other citations provided by Cochini, *Apostolic Origins*, 5–13.

65. Cf. 1 Cor 7:8–9, where Paul specifically identifies the inability to live continently as a reason for widows to remarry. As Heid points out (*Celibacy in the Early Church*, 54), the pastoral letters' concern that ministerial candidates must have demonstrated success as masters of households (1 Tm 3:4–5, 12; Ti 1:5–6) stands in some tension with Paul's recommendation of celibacy precisely to be free of household responsibilities in 1 Corinthians 7:32–34. But if his interpretation is correct, then the pastoral letters reflect an expectation that the ordained minister "without giving up his station in life, nevertheless for the sake of his new ministry would set aside the care of his own *oikos* and leave the responsibility to the lady of the house (*domina*) or to the steward, in order to devote himself entirely to the interests of the local church" (Heid, *Celibacy in the Early Church*, 55).

66. See the citations in McGovern, *Priestly Celibacy Today*, 91–92. For alternative interpretations, see Peter Gorday, ed., *Colossians, 1–2 Thessalonians, 1–2 Timothy, Titus, Philemon*, Ancient Christian Commentary on Scripture (Downer's Grove, IL: InterVarsity, 2000), 170–71, 286–87.

67. See de la Potterie, "Biblical Foundations," 22–25; Montague, *First and Second Timothy, Titus*, 75.

68. As Thomas Aquinas recognized, "This [stipulation] was made not merely for the sake of continence but because of the representation of the sacrament, because the spouse of the Church is Christ, and the Church is one" (*Commentary on 1 Timothy 3:1*).

69. In the West, this was regarded as a permanent discipline; in the East, as a temporary one at those times when the divine liturgy would be celebrated.

3: The Origins and Practice of Priestly Celibacy in the Early Church

1. An earlier version of this chapter was delivered at St. Joseph's Seminary, Dunwoodie, New York, in November of 2009 and printed in the *Dunwoodie Review* 33 (2010): 127–39. Some parts of that version are used here, with the permission of the copyright holder. The following abbreviations are used for series titles: ACW = Ancient Christian Writers; ANF = Ante-Nicene Fathers; CCL = Corpus christianorum, series latina; CSEL = Corpus Scriptorum Ecclesiasticorum Latinorum; FOTC = Fathers of the Church; GCS = Die griechischen christlichen Schriftsteller; NPNF = Nicene and Post-Nicene Fathers; PG = Patrologia graeca; and PL = Patrologia latina. Translations not otherwise identified are my own.

2. See particularly canons 12 and 13 of the Council in Trullo, or the Quini-sext, held in 692 (translation in NPNF 2, 14, 370–72). Pope Benedict XVI, in the postsynodal apostolic exhortation *Sacramentum caritatis*, 24, wrote, "The Synod Fathers wished to emphasize that the ministerial priesthood, through ordina-tion, calls for complete configuration to Christ. While respecting the different practice and tradition of the Eastern Churches, there is a need to reaffirm the profound meaning of priestly celibacy, which is rightly considered a priceless treasure, and is also confirmed by the Eastern practice of choosing Bishops only from the ranks of the celibate." See also Peter L'Huillier, "Episcopal Celibacy in the Orthodox Tradition," *St. Vladimir's Theological Quarterly* 35 (1991): 271–300; John Behr, "Reflections upon Episcopal Celibacy," *St. Vladimir's Theological Quar-terly* 36 (1992): 141–48; and Peter L'Huillier, "Archbishop Peter's Answer to the 'Reflections upon Episcopal Celibacy,'" *St. Vladimir's Theological Quarterly* 36 (1992): 149–51.

3. Gustav Bickell, "Der Cölibat eine apostolische Anordnung," *Zeitschrift für katholische Theologie* 2 (1878): 26–64.

4. Franz Xaver Funk, "Der Cölibat keine apostolische Anordnung," *Theolo-gische Quartalschrift* 61 (1879): 208–47.

5. Gustav Bickell, "Der Cölibat dennoch eine apostolische Anordnung," *Zeitschrift für katholische Theologie* 3 (1879): 792–99.

6. Franz Xaver Funk, "Der Cölibat noch lange keine apostolische Anord-nung," *Theologische Quartalschrift* 62 (1880): 202–21.

7. See Stanley L. Jaki, *Theology of Priestly Celibacy* (Front Royal, VA: Christen-dom Press, 1997), 6–7.

8. For example, Jean-Paul Audet, *Mariage et célibat dans le service pastoral de l'église: Histoire et orientations* (Paris: Editions de l'Orante, 1967), trans. Rosemary Sheed as *Structures of Christian Priesthood: A Study of Home, Marriage, and Celibacy in the Pastoral Service of the Church* (New York: Macmillan, 1968); Roger Gryson, *Les origines du célibat ecclésiastique du premier au septième siècle* (Gembloux, Bel-gium: Duculot, 1970); Edward Schillebeeckx, *Het ambts-celibaat in de branding* (Bilthoven, Netherlands: H. Nelissen, 1966), trans. C. A. L. Jarrott as *Celibacy* (New York: Sheed & Ward, 1968).

9. William E. Phipps, *Clerical Celibacy: The Heritage* (New York: Continuum, 2004).

10. Ibid., 2–3.

11. Christian Cochini, *Origines apostoliques du célibat sacerdotal* (Paris: Éditions Lethielleux, 1981).

12. Cochini, *Apostolic Origins*.

13. Stickler, *The Case for Clerical Celibacy*.

14. Stefan Heid, *Zölibat in der frühen Kirche: Die Anfänge einer Enthaltsamkeitsp-flicht für Kleriker in Ost und West* (Paderborn, Germany: Ferdinand Schöningh, 1997).

15. Heid, *Celibacy in the Early Church*.

16. Cochini, *Apostolic Origins*, 438.

17. Heid, *Celibacy in the Early Church*, 57.

18. Ibid., 48–50.

19. St. Cyril of Jerusalem, *Catechetical Orations* 4, 26: "Let not those who have been married only once find fault with those who have indulged in a second

marriage. For, while continence is a noble and admirable thing, it is also allowable to enter upon a second marriage, that the weak may not commit fornication" (in *Works of Saint Cyril of Jerusalem*, trans. Leo P. McCauley and Anthony A. Stephenson, 2 vols., FOTC 61 and 64 [Washington, DC: Catholic University of America, 1969–70], 1, 132).

20. Clement of Alexandria, *Stromata* 3, 18, 108, 2: "What reply to these directions have those who recoil from intercourse and birth? For he also lays down that the bishop who is to rule the Church must be a man who governs his own household well. A household pleasing to the Lord consists of a marriage with one wife" (in *Alexandrian Christianity*, trans. John E. L. Oulton and Henry Chadwick, Library of Christian Classics [Philadelphia: Westminster Press, 1954], 91).

21. John Chrysostom, *Homilies on Titus* 2 (on Titus 1:6): "Why does he bring forward such an one? To stop the mouths of those heretics, who condemned marriage, showing that it is not an unholy thing in itself, but so far honorable, that a married man might ascend the holy throne; and at the same time reproving the wanton, and not permitting their admission into this high office who contracted a second marriage. . . . For you all know, that though it is not forbidden by the laws to enter into a second marriage, yet it is a thing liable to many ill constructions" (in *Saint Chrysostom: Homilies on . . . Titus*, ed. Philip Schaff, NPNF 1, 13 [repr., Grand Rapids, MI: Eerdmans, 1976], 524).

22. Ambrose, letter 63 to the church at Vercelli, 63: "I have not passed over this point, because many persons contend that the husband of one wife has reference to the time after baptism, so that any impediment which would ensue would be washed away in baptism. Indeed, all faults and sins are washed away, so that, if one has polluted his body by many whom he has not bound to himself by the marriage law, these are all forgiven him. But the marriages are not done away with if he has made a second contract, for sin, not the law, is loosed by the laver [of baptism]" (in *Saint Ambrose: Letters*, trans. Mary Melchior Beyenka, FOTC 26 [New York: Fathers of the Church, 1954], 344).

23. Jerome, *Commentary on Titus* 1:6 (PL 26, 564–65). In this passage, Jerome argues forcefully that a second marriage is not always to be rejected. A young man who married twice and was quickly left a widower practices continence better than a man in a long and active marriage. To have two wives at once is forbidden. A man widowed before baptism who marries again after baptism is not excluded from the priesthood. It is better to have married twice than to have fornicated with prostitutes. Second marriages are permitted to laymen. Since no English translation exists, it may help to provide one. "But we should understand what he says, 'the husband of one wife,' in this way: that we should not think that every man married once is better than one married twice. Rather, he who puts himself forward as an example in his teaching can encourage monogamy and continence. Take as an example a young man who lost his wife and, overcome by the needs of the flesh, took a second wife. He immediately loses her and then lives continently. Another man remains married right up to old age and never ceases to have relations with his wife (which many understand as happiness), or leave off the deeds of the flesh. Which of the two seems to you to be better, more modest, more continent? Surely he who was unhappy even in his second marriage, and was converted and lived in modesty and holiness, and not he who was not separated from the embrace of his wife even in his old age. So anyone who

is elected as once married should not congratulate himself on the grounds that he is better than any man married twice. In him, happiness was chosen rather than strength of will. Some think thus about this passage: it was Jewish custom, they say, to have either two wives, or many. We read this in the Old Law about Abraham and Jacob. And now they want this to be the law, that the man who is to be elected a bishop should not have two wives at one time. Many people much more superstitiously than honestly think that even those who, when they were Gentiles and had one wife, and lost her, and after baptism into Christ married another, should not be chosen for the priesthood. If this is to be observed, those who previously exercised their unbounded libido with prostitutes should be kept out of the episcopacy more than those who were baptized and married one wife. It is much more detestable to have fornicated with many women than to be found twice married. In the one man, the unhappiness of matrimony exists, in the other the licentiousness that leads to sin. Montanus, and those who follow the schism of Novatian, presumed the name of purity for themselves. They think that second marriages should be forbidden to members of the Church. Since the Apostle mandates this practice for bishops and presbyters, surely he mitigated it for the rest. It is not that he encourages second marriages, but he concedes the necessities of the flesh. Tertullian, too, wrote a heretical book, *On Monogamy*. No one who has read the Apostle will not realize that Tertullian contradicts the Apostle. And indeed: it is in our own power to allow a bishop or a priest to have one wife, without transgressing."

24. Theodore of Mopsuestia, *Commentary on 1 Timothy*: "For they [i.e., various interpreters] say that Paul has spoken thus, so that any man who is brought forward to be a bishop and has taken a wife will live chastely with her, being content with her alone as the recipient of his natural desires. Likewise any man who lives on after the death of his first wife may legitimately take a second wife, as long as he lives in the same way with her as with the first, and ought not be prohibited from becoming a bishop. They say that Paul has laid down a canon here. I accept this view, although I am not persuaded that he lays down a specific rule with regard to the second matter, i.e., that of the eligibility of remarried men for the episcopal office" (in *Colossians, 1–2 Thessalonians, 1–2 Timothy, Titus, Philemon*, ed. Peter Gorday, Ancient Christian Commentary on Scripture, New Testament 9 [Downers Grove, IL: InterVarsity, 2000], 170).

25. Basil the Great, letter 188, 12: "The canon absolutely excludes from the ministry those who are twice married" (in *Saint Basil: Letters*, 2, trans. Agnes Clare Way, FOTC 28 [New York: Fathers of the Church, 1955], 23).

26. Ambrose, letter 63, 63: "The Apostle laid down the law saying: 'If anyone is without reproach, the husband of one wife.' Whoever, then, is without reproach, the husband of one wife, is included among those held by the law to be qualified for the priesthood, but he who entered a second marriage has not the guilt of pollution, though he is disqualified from the privilege of the priesthood" (344).

27. John Chrysostom, *Homilies on 1 Timothy* 10: "'A Bishop, then,' he says, 'must be blameless, the husband of one wife.' This he does not set down as a rule, as if he must not be without one, but as prohibiting his having more than one" (in *Saint Chrysostom: Homilies on . . . Timothy*, ed. Philip Schaff, NPNF 1, 13 [repr., Grand Rapids, MI: Eerdmans, 1976], 438).

28. Tertullian, *Exhortation to Chastity*, 7: "With us the law which requires that none but monogamists are to be chosen for the order of the priesthood, is more comprehensive in its scope and exacting in its details [than the Old Testament]. So true is this that, as I recall, there have been men deposed from office for digamy" (in *Tertullian: Treatises on Marriage and Remarriage*, trans. William P. Le Saint, ACW 13 [Westminster, MD: Newman, 1951], 53).

29. *Constitutions of the Holy Apostles* 6, 3, 17: "We have already said, that a bishop, a presbyter, and a deacon, when they are constituted, must be but once married, whether their wives be alive or whether they be dead; and that it is not lawful for them, if they are unmarried when they are ordained, to be married afterwards; or if they be then married, to marry a second time, but to be content with that wife which they had when they came to ordination" (in *Fathers of the Third and Fourth Centuries*, ed. James Donaldson, ANF 7 [repr., Grand Rapids, MI: Eerdmans, 1975], 457).

30. Appeal is sometimes made to *Didascalia Apostolorum* 10 as an early witness to clerical continence. In R. Hugh Connolly's translation from Syriac the passage reads, "But it is required that the bishop be thus: 'a man that hath taken one wife, that hath governed his house well.' And thus let him be proved when he receives the imposition of hands to sit in the office of the bishopric: whether he be chaste, and whether his wife also be a believer and chaste; and whether he has brought up his children in the fear of God, and admonished and taught them" (R. Hugh Connolly, ed., *Didascalia Apostolorum: The Syriac Version Translated and Accompanied by the Verona Latin Fragments* [Oxford, UK: Clarendon, 1929], 32. The sense of "chaste" here seems too vague to imply obligatory continence. There is a critical edition of the Latin version: Erik Tidner, ed., *Didascaliae Apostolorum, Canonum ecclesiasticorum, Traditionis apostolicae versiones Latinae*, Texte und Untersuchungen 75 (Berlin: Akademie, 1963), 17–18. In the Latin, the candidate is to have educated his children *caste*, "chastely," which also suggests a more general sense for the word.

3. Eusebius of Caesarea, *Demonstratio evangelica* 1, 9, in *The Proof of the Gospel*, trans. W. J. Ferrar, 1 (repr., Grand Rapids, MI: Baker, 1981), 53–54, altered. The translation cited has "after ordination," for *loipon*, which is not so specific.

32. Ambrosiaster, *Commentarius in epistulas Paulinas*, on 1 Timothy 3:12, 3, ed. H. J. Vogels, CSEL 81/3 (Vienna: Holder-Pichler-Tempsky, 1969), 269.

33. Ambrose, letter 63, 62, in *Concerning Virgins*, trans. H. de Romestin, NPNF 2, 10 (repr., Grand Rapids, MI: Eerdmans, 1976), 465, altered. Beyenka's translation in FOTC 26 is less clear here.

34. Epiphanius, *Panarion* 59, 4, 1, ed. Karl Holl, GCS 31 (Berlin: Akademie, 1980), 367. Epiphanius directs this section against the Cathari, who wanted to forbid second marriages to all Christians. The following sentence in the text states that in some places priests, deacons, and subdeacons still father children.

35. Christians of the first four or five centuries often counseled against a second marriage for a man who had been widowed—for all Christian men, not only clerics—but they seldom if ever opposed it. To give a few examples, the Greek apologist Athenagoras, in the second century, writes that Christians should either remain unmarried or contract only one marriage, for "a second marriage is gilded adultery" (*Legatio* 33, 4, in *Athenagoras:* Legatio *and* De resurrectione, trans. William R. Schoedel, Oxford Early Christian Texts [Oxford, UK: Clarendon,

1972], 81). A man who turns away from his wife for another woman, even if his wife had died, is a covert adulterer (33, 6, p. 81). Basil the Great, in his canonical letters (letters 188, 199, and 217, addressed to Amphilochius of Iconium), imposes one or two years' penance on a Christian who has contracted a second marriage and three or four years penance—although Basil himself prefers five—for a third marriage (Basil, letter 188, 4). A cleric who marries a second time is excluded from the ministry (12). Elsewhere in these letters, Basil writes that a third marriage pollutes the Church (letter 199, canon 50, in Basil, *Saint Basil: Letters*).

36. Origen, *Homilies on Luke* 6, 1, trans. Joseph T. Lienhard, FOTC 94 (Washington, DC: Catholic University of America, 1996), 23.

37. Pope Paul VI, "Sacerdotalis Caelibatus," 35–36.

38. See Tertullian, *De exhortatione castitatis*, 13 (PL 2, 930); St. Epiphanius, *Adversus Haereses* II, 48, 9 and 59, 4 (PG 41, 869, 1025); St. Ephrem, *Carmina nisibena*, XVIII, XIX, ed. G. Bickell (Leipzig, Germany: Brockhaus, 1866), 122; Eusebius of Caesarea, *Demonstratio evangelica* 1, 9 (PG 22, 81); St. Cyril of Jerusalem, *Catechesis* 12, 25 (PG 33, 757); St. Ambrose, *De officiis ministrorum* 1, 50 (PL 16, 97–98); St. Augustine, *De moribus Ecclesiae catholicae* 1, 32 (PL 32, 1339); St. Jerome, *Adversus Vigilantium*, 2 (PL 23, 340–41); Bishop Synesius of Ptolemais, *Epistula* 105 (PG 66, 1485).

39. First done at the Council of Elvira, ca. 300, canon 33 (Mansi II, 11).

40. Session XXIV, canons 9–10.

41. Canon 132, §1 (Code of 1917).

42. See, for example, Cyprian of Carthage, letter 63, 14, in *Saint Cyprian: Letters*, trans. Rose Bernard Donna, FOTC 51 (Washington, DC: Catholic University of America, 1964), 212–13.

43. Tertullian, *On the Veiling of Virgins*, 10: "Nor, similarly, (is [the veiling of virgins] permitted) on the ground of any distinction whatever. Otherwise, it were sufficiently discourteous, that while females, subjected as they are throughout to men, bear in their front an honorable mark of their virginity, whereby they may be looked up to and gazed at on all sides and magnified by the brethren, so many men-virgins, so many voluntary eunuchs, should carry their glory in secret, carrying no token to make them, too, illustrious" (in *Fathers of the Third Century*, trans. S. Thelwall, ANF 4 [repr., Grand Rapids, MI: Eerdmans, 1976], 33).

44. Tertullian, *Exhortation to Chastity*, 13: "With a little effort you could illustrate this over and over again from the lives of our own women. Such examples will be better, too, than those I have already mentioned [i.e., Lucretia, who committed suicide after she was violated], since it is much more remarkable to live in chastity than it is to die for it. It is easier to lay down your life because you have lost something you valued than it is to keep on living in order to protest something for which you would gladly die. How many men and women there are whose chastity has obtained for them the honor of ecclesiastical orders! How many who have chosen to be wedded to God! How many who have restored to their flesh the honor it had lost! They have already set themselves apart as children of the world to come by killing concupiscence and, with it, all else that has no place in Paradise! Therefore, we must conclude that those who wish to enter Paradise ought, at long last, to put an end to a way of life which is not found in Paradise" (63–64).

45. Cyprian of Carthage, *On the Dress of Virgins*, 4, in *Saint Cyprian: Treatises*, trans. Angela Elizabeth Keenan, FOTC 36 (New York: Fathers of the Church, 1958), 34. The text continues, "But since woman is a part of man and was taken and formed from him, almost universally in the Scriptures God addresses the first formed because they are two in one flesh, and in the man is signified likewise the woman."

46. Ibid.

47. St. Augustine, *Holy Virginity* 18, 18, in *Saint Augustine: Treatises on Marriage and Other Subjects*, trans. John McQuade, FOTC 27 (New York: Fathers of the Church, 1955), 160.

48. St. Augustine, *Confessions* 8, 6, 15.

49. See Jerome, letters 108 and 127.

50. See St. Augustine, *On the Catholic and Manichean Ways of Life* 1, 33, 70.

51. St. Ambrose, *Hexameron* 3, 5, 23.

52. Rutilius Claudius Namatianus, *De reditu suo*, 439–52.

53. Sulpicius Severus, *Life of St. Martin* 10, 9.

54. See Arthur Cooper Cooper-Marsdin, *The History of the Islands of the Lerins: The Monastery, Saints and Theologians of S. Honorat* (Cambridge: Cambridge University Press, 1913).

55. Council of Elvira, canon 33: "It pleased us to command, absolutely, bishops, priests, and deacons, and all clerics assigned to ministry, to abstain from their wives and not to beget children. But let whoever does so be deposed from the honor of the clergy" (José Vives, *Concilios Visigóticos e Hispano-Romanos* [Barcelona: Consejo Superior de Investigaciones Científicas, 1963], 7).

56. Canon 29, from the Synod of Arles, is one of six canons found only in a small number of manuscripts of this council, and their authenticity is suspect. The editor entitles them "canones suppositii" or "unauthentic canons." A full translation of the canon: "Moreover, as is worthy, moderate, and decent, we urge the brethren that priests and deacons should not cohabit with their wives, because they are concerned with daily ministry. Let whoever acts against this norm be deposed from the honor of the clergy" (C. Munier, ed., *Concilia Galliae A. 314-A. 506*, CCL 148 [Turnhout, Belgium: Brepols, 1963], 25).

57. See M. Migne, "Concile ou collection d'Elvira," *Revue d'histoire eccésiastique* 70 (1975): 361–87, who holds that only the first twenty-one canons were enacted at Elvira.

58. Pope Siricius, letter 1, *Directa ad decessorem* 7, 8 (PL 13, 1138B).

59. Ibid., 7, 10 (PL 13, 1139A).

60. Pope Siricius, letter 5, *Cum in unum*, 3 (PL 13, 1160A). Text of the Roman synod of 386 is also printed in *Concilia Africae A. 345-A. 525*, ed. C. Munier, CCL 149 (Turnhout, Belgium: Brepols, 1974), 61.

61. Ibid.

62. Second Council of Carthage 2 (CCL 149, 13).

63. Pope Innocent I, letter 6, *Consulenti tibi* 1, 2 (PL 20, 496B).

64. Pope Siricius, letter *Directa ad decessorem* 9, 13 (PL 13, 1142–43). Since no English version exists, it may be helpful to provide a full translation: "So anyone who dedicates himself to the service of the Church from his childhood should be baptized before the age of puberty and installed in the ministry of lector. If he lives honorably from the beginning of his adolescence up to the thirtieth year of

his age, and is content with only one wife (and he married her as a virgin, by the common blessing given through a priest), he ought to be made an acolyte and a subdeacon. Let him accede later to the rank of deacon, if he first proves that he is worthy by his previous continence. If he ministers for five years more in a praiseworthy manner, the office of presbyter should fittingly follow. From there, he will be able to attain the episcopal chair after ten years, if the integrity of his life and faith were approved throughout these times." The key phrase, "si se ipse primitus continentia praeeunte dignum probarit," is difficult. David G. Hunter translates it "if thereafter he maintains the level of his previous continence." With hesitation, I have written "if he first proves that he is worthy by his previous continence," but it is unclear when Siricius holds that the practice of continence should begin. (David G. Hunter, *Marriage, Celibacy, and Heresy in Ancient Christianity: The Jovinianist Controversy* [Oxford: Oxford University Press, 2007], 211).

65. Hunter, *Marriage, Celibacy*, esp. 213–19.

66. See *Gaudium et Spes* 48, §1; *Catechism of the Catholic Church* 1601.

67. The Fathers wrote many treatises on virginity. The most important ones that are available in English translations are these: Tertullian, *On the Veiling of Virgins*, 27–37; Cyprian, *On the Dress of Virgins*, 31–52; Methodius, *Symposium: A Treatise on Chastity*, trans. Herbert Musurillo, ACW 27 (Westminster, MD: Newman Press, 1958); St. Gregory of Nyssa, *On Virginity*, trans. William More and Henry Austin Wilson, NPNF 2, 5, 343–71; John Chrysostom, *On Virginity: Against Remarriage*, trans. S. R. Shore (Lewiston, NY: Mellen, 1983); Ambrose, *Concerning Virgins*, 363-87; Ambrose, *On Virginity*, trans. Daniel Callam (Toronto: Peregrina, 1989); and St. Augustine, *Holy Virginity*, 143–212.

68. Cyprian, *On the Dress of Virgins*, 50.

69. St. Augustine, *Holy Virginity* 13, 13, p. 155.

70. St. Augustine, *Holy Virginity* 2, 2, p. 145.

71. Cyprian, letter 63. See also Second Vatican Council, *Lumen gentium* 21, note 22.

72. St. Augustine, *Holy Virginity* 35, 35, p. 185.

73. Pope Benedict XVI, "The Church Movements and Their Place in Theology," in *The Pilgrim Fellowship of Faith: The Church as Communion* (San Francisco: Ignatius, 2005), 180. A recently ordained Jesuit priest, Father Aaron Pidel, S.J., commented, "The struggle to maintain priestly celibacy is, for Benedict, precisely the struggle *against* the institutionalization of the Church—a struggle 'lest [the institutional structure] harden into an armor that stifles her actual spiritual life.' I suspect that many proponents of a married clergy would resonate with Benedict's anti-institutional sentiments. Few, it seems, are far-sighted enough to anticipate that married clergy would not be the undoing of clerical control, but its final victory" ("The End of Celibacy?" Whosoever Desires, October 25, 2009, http://whosoeverdesires.wordpress.com/).

74. St. Gregory of Nyssa, *On Virginity*, 24, p. 371.

4: Configured to Christ

1. Rite of Ordination of a Deacon, 227.

2. Cf. Rule of St Augustine 1.8: superbia vero etiam in bonis operibus insidiatur ut pereant.

3. On the relationship between the human and spiritual dimensions of formation with particular reference to priesthood, cf. James Keating, "Christ Is the Sure Foundation: Priestly Human Formation Completed in and by Spiritual Formation," *Vetera et Nova*, 8 (2010): 883–99.

4. John Paul II, *Redemptor Hominis*, 8, building his reflections on the theological anthropology found in *Gaudium et Spes*, 22. Joseph Ratzinger had also noted and developed this idea in his *Introduction to Christianity* (San Francisco: Ignatius, 2004), 210–12, from lectures he had given and originally published in 1968.

5. John Paul II, *Pastores Dabo Vobis*, 43; cf. *Presbyterorum Ordinis*, 3.

6. Cf. 1 John 1.

7. Cf. Irenaeus, *Adversus Haereses*, 4.6.3: *Agnitio Patris est Filii manifestatio*; Origen, *De principiis*, 1.2.6: *Revelat [Patrem] autem per hoc quod ipse intellegitur*.

8. In addition to the classic biography of Francis Trochu, *The Curé d'Ars: St. Jean-Marie-Baptiste Vianney* (Charlotte, NC: Tan, 2009), cf. George William Rutler, *The Curé of Ars Today* (San Francisco: Ignatius, 1988), who notes, "Not by authority or the privilege of authority did the Curé command such attention. Anyone there was witness to the trust he engendered, and he won the common trust by winning individual hearts. . . . By showing the people, even the youngest of the people, himself, he displayed the universal love of which the priest is mediator. . . . By being a true priest, the Curé engendered the trust of souls who had come close to losing the very sense of place in the world" (154).

9. Cf. Ratzinger, *Introduction to Christianity*, 228–34.

10. United States Conference of Catholic Bishops (USCCB), *Program of Priestly Formation*, 5th ed. (Washington, DC: Author, 2006), 79.

11. Pope John Paul II, *Pastores Dabo Vobis*, 43–44, March 25, 1992.

12. USCCB, *Program of Priestly Formation*, 77; cf. 1 Thessalonians 5:23, the lectio brevis of Compline each Thursday.

13. Pope Paul VI, *Optatam Totius*, 10, October 28, 1965.

14. Cf. Pope John Paul II, His General Audience of July 14, 1993.

15. Athanasius, in his *De Incarnatione Verbi* and Thomas in the Third Part of his *Summa Theologiae*.

16. One can refer to the important work done, for example, by Msgr. Stephen J. Rossetti, *Why Priests Are Happy: A Study of the Psychological and Spiritual Health of Priests* (Notre Dame, IN: Ave Maria Press, 2011).

17. Edwin O'Connor, *The Edge of Sadness* (Chicago: Loyola University Press, 2005). Published originally in 1961, it won the Pulitzer Prize in 1962.

18. Ibid., 380–81.

19. Ibid., 223.

20. Ibid., 352.

21. Aelred Squire, *Asking the Fathers* (London: SPCK, 1994), 115; John Paul offers much the same insight relative to human freedom in *Pastores Dabo Vobis*, 36.

22. St. Augustine, *Confessions* 1.1.

23. The early apologist Clement of Alexandria (ca. AD 215), who had many positive things to say about the married state, had also worried that celibacy, and the absence of spousal and familial demands, might make one irresponsible; cf. *Stromata* 7.70; cf. Clement of Alexandria, *Alexandrian Christianity*, 137–38. I am grateful to Father Joseph Lienhard, S.J., for this reference.

24. USCCB, *Program of Priestly Formation*, 80.

25. The Orthodox liturgiologist Alexander Schmemann quipped quite accurately, "Of all accusations against Christians, the most terrible one was uttered by Nietzsche, when he said that Christians had no joy" (*Sacraments and Orthodoxy* [New York: Herder and Herder, 1965], 27); G. K. Chesterton's peroration in *Orthodoxy* claimed that "joy, which was the small publicity of the pagan, is the gigantic secret of the Christian" ([San Francisco: Ignatius, 1995], 167). In the early fifth century, Augustine, in offering advice and encouragement to the Carthaginian deacon Deogratias had indicated that the essential component of effective catechesis is the joy (laetitia, hilaritas) the catechist discovers in the faith and witnesses personally to others; cf. Augustine's *De catechizandis rudibus*, prologue.

26. On the context and significance of this, cf. Mette B. Bruun, *Parables: Mapping Bernard of Clairvaux's Spiritual Topography* (Leiden, Netherlands: Brill, 2007), 222.

27. *Compendium of the Catechism of the Catholic Church*, 489.

28. John Paul II, *Pastores Dabo Vobis*, 44.

29. Cf. St. Augustine, *Confessions* 7.18.24.

30. François-Xavier Durrwell, *In the Redeeming Christ*, trans. Rosemary Sheed (London: Sheed & Ward, 1963); originally published in 1960 as *Dans le Christ Rédempteur: Notes de vie spirituelle*, it was reprinted twice in English, the last in 1968.

31. Ibid., 5.

32. Ibid., 5–8.

33. As Alexander Schmemann describes it, "This is not an 'other' world, different from the one God has created and given to us. It is our same world, already perfected in Christ, but not yet in us" (*For the Life of the World* [Crestwood, NY: St. Vladimir's Seminary Press, 2004], 42).

34. Cf. Ignace de la Potterie, *The Hour of Jesus: The Passion and the Resurrection of Jesus according to John* (New York: Alba House, 1990).

5: The Virginity of Jesus and the Celibacy of His Priests

1. This chapter builds upon earlier presentations I have made: two at symposia sponsored by the Institute for Priestly Formation, one in 2001 ("Renewed Celibate Living for Heralds of the New Evangelization") and the second in 2007 ("Christ's Virginal Heart and His Priestly Charity"); the third was at a conference convoked at St. John's Seminary, Brighton, by Cardinal Sean O'Malley in 2009 ("Christ's Virginity: Model of Celibacy and Service for the Diocesan Priest"— hereafter, "Brighton Address"). The second and third are particularly apposite to this presentation.

2. Pope Benedict XVI, "The Eucharist and Priestly Celibacy," in Post-Synodal Apostolic Exhortation *Sacramentum caritatis* 24, February 22, 2007.

3. Hans Urs von Balthasar, "The Meaning of Celibacy," *Communio* 3 (1976): 321–22.

4. Pope Benedict XVI, "The Eucharist and Priestly Celibacy."

5. See Meier, *A Marginal Jew*. For another useful source, see Marco Adinolfi, "Il celibate di Gesù," *Bibbia e Oriente* 13, nos. 4–5 (1971): 145–58.

6. Meier, *A Marginal Jew*, 1:334, 335. In regard to the logion that there are "some who are eunuchs for the kingdom" (Mt 19:21), Meier holds that "it is

possible that Jesus refers to his total, all-consuming commitment to proclaiming and realizing the kingdom of God" (342).

7. Meier, *A Marginal Jew*, 1:345. In working out his reasoning, Meier takes as his foil William Phipps, *Was Jesus Married? The Distortion of Sexuality in the Christian Tradition* (New York: Harper & Row, 1970). According to Meier, Phipps argues that, without any explicit mention of Jesus' marital state in the New Testament, the positive attitudes toward marriage in the Palestinian Jewish society of Jesus' day should make one conclude he was very likely married. However, the elements of historical-critical methodology espoused by scholars characterized as engaged in the "third quest" would lead one to conclude that Phipps, while taking into account the similarity between Jesus and his social milieu, does not do justice to the sorts of discontinuity that belonged to Jesus' life precisely because of his "subversion" of the Judaism that had become the norm of his time. On this point, see N. T. Wright, *Jesus and the Victory of God*, vol. 2 of *Christian Origins and the Question of God* (Minneapolis: Fortress Press, 1999), 131–33.

8. For this attentive reading I take as my guide Angelo Amato, S.D.B., *Il celibato di Gesù* (Vatican City: Libreria Editrice Vatican, 2010). This short work is based on the text of an address delivered at the University of the Holy Cross, Rome, on March 4, 2010. By the kind permission of the author, the text was translated for limited private circulation by William Millea. All quotations here from this work are from that translation.

9. Amato, *Il celibato di Gesù*, 13, 15–16.

10. Mark 2:19–20 (cf., Matthew 9:14–17 and Luke 5:33–39); see also John 3:28–29.

11. N. T. Wright, in a formulation that is striking for its starkness, refers to this usage as "Israel-language" (*Jesus and the Victory of God*, 277). Wright sees that Jesus, by referring to himself as the bridegroom, is calling on his listeners to recognize that in his person he fulfills the expectation that the prophets had aroused in them, the definitive vindication of the chosen people by their God. See, for example, Hosea 1–3 and Ezekiel 16. Jesus' status as bridegroom is consistent with his frequently comparing the kingdom he inaugurates with a wedding feast. And, according to Wright, further confirmation of Jesus' self-understanding as the bridegroom of the People of God is found in his generous table fellowship at meals that both foreshadow and bring to pass the renewed marriage covenant of God and Israel (433–34).

12. See Amato, *Il celibato di Gesù*, 13–15.

13. See Wright, *Jesus and the Victory of God*, 466, 575.

14. Meier, *A Marginal Jew*, 1:342. Amato offers his reflection on the significance of this passage in the section of his work titled "Gesù e l' 'eunuchia,'" in *Il celibato di Gesù*, 17–23. See also, Jean Galot, S.J., "Il celibato sacerdotale alla luce del celibato di Cristo," *Civiltà Cattolica* 120 (1969): 3:367–70.

15. For a complete survey of sources, see Sebastian Tromp, S.J., "Articulus II: *Virginitas Christi*," in *Corpus Christi quod est Ecclesiae*, vol. 4, *De Virgine deipara Maria corde mistici corporis* (Rome: apud aedes Universitatis Gregorianae, 1972), 124–32. I am indebted to Jörgen Vijgen for bringing this source to my attention, through the kind offices of Romanus Cessario, O.P.

16. St. Jerome, "Christus virgo," *Epist.* 48, 21; PL 22: 510.

17. St. Thomas Aquinas, *In III Sententiae* 12, 3, 1, 1, 2: "Non assumpsit sexum ad usum sed ad perfectionem naturae." I am grateful for this reference to Paul Gondreau, who assisted me at the request of Romanus Cessario, O.P.

18. St. Thomas Aquinas, "Ipse [Christus] virginitatem servavit," *Summa theologiae*, II-II, 152, 4, resp.

19. "Propter conformitatem ad Christum sponsum, ad quem virgines conformes facit" (St. Bonaventure, *De perfectione evangelica* 3, 3).

20. St. Robert Bellarmine, "Virgo Mater perpetua et Christus Virgo perpetuus," cited in Tromp, "Articulus II," 126.

21. "Si sacerdotes, si religiosi viri mulieresque, si ii denique omnes, qui quavis ratione divino se devoverunt famulatui, perfectam castitatem colunt, idcirco hoc profecto evenit, quod Divinus eorum Magister virgo fuit ad suae usque vitae obitum" (Pius XII, *Sacra virginitas* 19, March 25, 1954). (Note that the paragraph numbering comes from the English translation on the Vatican web site and is not found in the Latin original.)

22. "Christus unicus Dei Filius, ob ipsam suam incarnationem, Mediator inter caelum et terram interque Patrem et genus humanum est constitutus. Cui prorsus congruens muneri, Christus per totius vitae cursum in virginitatis condicione est versatus; qua quidem re significatur, eum totum se devovisse Dei hominumque ministerio" (Paul VI, *Sacerdotalis caelibatus* 21, June 24, 1967).

23. "Ipse Christus quosdam invitavit ut Eum in hoc sequerentur vitae genere, cuius Ipse permanet exemplar" (*Catechism of the Catholic Church* 1618).

24. Second Vatican Council, *Lumen gentium* (*LG*), "Consilia . . . praesertim ad genus vitae virginalis ac pauperis, quod sibi elegit Christus Dominus, quodque Mater Eius Virgo amplexa est, hominem christianum magis conformare valent" (46). "Consilia evangelica castitatis Deo dicatae, paupertatis et oboedientiae, utpote in verbis et exemplis Domini fundata" (43). In regard to the passage from *LG* 46, it is worthy of note that Tromp is critical of describing Jesus' virginity as "*chosen*" ("Articulus II," 130).

25. Bertrand de Margerie, *Christ for the World—The Heart of the Lamb: A Treatise on Christology*, trans. Malachy Carroll (Chicago: Franciscan Herald Press, 1973), 336.

26. First Vatican Council, *Enchiridion symbolorum et definitionum* (*DS*) 3016. On the theological method of deepening the understanding of Revelation through articulating the connections between its mysteries, the *Catechism of the Catholic Church* gives us, as Pope John Paul II said it would, a sure point of reference. The *Catechism* observes that "Christ's whole earthly life—his words and deeds, his silences and sufferings, indeed his manner of being and speaking—s Revelation of the Father" (516). And so, his virginity is certainly worthy of our attempt to understand it more deeply; and these efforts will undoubtedly bear good fruit insofar as we are directed by the grace of the Holy Spirit.

27. "That such is the case in the covenant between God and Israel is the clear teaching of the prophets, as they build upon this basic theme already found in the Law. I would offer as a prime exemplification of this fact the classic pericope from the sixteenth chapter of the Prophet Ezekiel (16:1–63). As you recall, it is in this passage that God speaks so poignantly of having found Israel weltering in her own blood and of his compassion that led him to wash her and make her his very own bride. The sense of marriage as the originary paradigm for God's

relationship with his Holy People, as we see it foreshadowed in the Old Testament, finds what could be claimed as its clearest New Testament expression in the fifth chapter of St. Paul's Letter to the Ephesians (Eph 5:22–33). There St. Paul, after outlining the sort of relationship that should exist in a marriage, says, 'I mean that this is a great mystery in Christ's relationship to the Church' (Eph 5:32)" ("Brighton Address," 8).

28. "Brighton Address," 10.

29. Ibid.

30. "The ministerial or hierarchical priesthood of bishops and priests, and the common priesthood of all the faithful participate, 'each in its own proper way, in the one priesthood of Christ.' While being 'ordered one to another,' they differ essentially (*LG*, n. 10.2). In what sense? While the common priesthood of the faithful is exercised by the unfolding of baptismal grace—a life of faith, hope, and charity, a life according to the Spirit—the ministerial priesthood is at the service of the common priesthood" (*CCC*, 1547).

31. These two parts of a priest's being—participation and presence—are what some phenomenologists call "moments," that is nondetachable parts. Phenomenological philosophy has the resources to explicate further that each part functions as ground for the other. To be a participant is a way to be a part, and being a part accounts for being a presentation. Or, to look at from the side of presentation, to be a presentation of something is to form a whole with it. See Robert Sokolowski, "Parts and Wholes," in *Husserlian Meditations: How Words Present Things* (Evanston, IL: Northwestern University Press, 1974), 8–17. On parts and wholes (identity and difference) accounting for and being accounted for by presentation (presence and absence), see Sokolowski, "First Philosophy: Analysis of Being as Being," in *Presence and Absence: A Philosophical Investigation of Language and Being* (Bloomington: Indiana University Press, 1978), 157–71. For an example of employing the resources of phenomenological philosophy in the effort to advance the *intellectus fidei* in regard to Holy Orders, see Sokolowski, "The Identity of the Bishop: A Study in the Theology of Disclosure," in *Christian Faith and Human Understanding: Studies on the Eucharist, Trinity and the Human Person* (Washington, DC: Catholic University of America Press, 2006), 113–30.

32. This same point was made by Pope Benedict's predecessor, Paul VI, in *Sacerdotalis caelibatus*, nn. 38–40.

33. On this point I am employing a distinction made by Father Donald Keefe. See "Brighton Address," 12: "Keefe points out that some things belong together 'essentially' but not 'necessarily.' To say that being a priest and being celibate belong together essentially is to assert that their bond is not extrinsic, incidental, an accident or artificial. They are not held together by some act of the arbitrary will of authority. Rather, the nature of each is a complement to the other. The pair forms an integral whole in which each reinforces, heightens and perfects the being of the other. To say that their belonging together, while essential, is not necessary is to say that, although it is right for them to be together, the priesthood may be detached from the celibate state which perfects it. It may be given to a married man. Keefe calls this sort of disjunction an 'accommodation.' Accommodations are such that it is the normal practice in the Eastern Churches to admit married men to the priesthood; and, it is an accommodation that married men, in some instances, are admitted to the priesthood even in the Latin Church.

However, all the Churches, East and West agree that those in the rank of "high priest," which is to say, bishops, must all be celibate. And this is not merely for pragmatic reasons but for mystagogical and sacramental reasons." On the topic of the meaning of requiring that bishops be celibate in the Eastern Churches, see Peter L'Huillier, "Episcopal Celibacy in the Orthodox Tradition." See also Behr, "Reflections upon Episcopal Celibacy," and L'Huillier's response to Behr, "Archbishop Peter's Answer." L'Huillier sets as one of his goals "to discover the reasons underlying this development," that is, promoting only celibates to the episcopacy (292). In working to that end he never mentions the virginity of Jesus; rather, he asserts that "the requirement of episcopal celibacy has no *dogmatic* significance" (297, emphasis mine). In view of the Church's belief in Jesus' virginity, this seems surprising. (I am grateful to Father Joseph Lienhard, S.J., for bringing these references to my attention.)

34. See Romans 5:12–21; 8:21; 1 Corinthians 15:20–21; 2 Corinthians 5:17; Colossians 1:15; and John 19:33–35.

35. See, for example, the work of Bertrand de Margerie, S.J., who has a chapter titled, "The Mystery of Human Sexuality: The Priestly Celibacy of Christ" in his *Christ for the World*, 313–39. In this chapter de Margerie states that through his sacrificial love as the Lamb of God, Christ, who is the creator of human sexuality, divinizes and redeems this essential aspect of the human person through his priestly celibacy.

36. Von Balthasar affirms that celibacy is not "an" eschatological sign; rather, "it is 'the' eschatological sign, and as such it becomes indispensable." He goes on to explain his preference for the definite article over the indefinite in this formulation by considering how in the new covenant sexuality comes to be valued in a new way: "The new and eternal covenant values sexuality entirely differently from the old one. In the old covenant it pertained to the messianic hope, as the book of Tobit reaches us with great delicacy. But with the birth of Christ from the Virgin Mary, with Jesus' virginal life, with his death, his descent to hell and his resurrection from the dead, a totally new theological situation has arisen. Sexuality has arrived at its internal end; the continuance of the race has reached a certain theological insignificance" ("The Meaning of Celibacy," 325).

37. Thus the glorified body of Christ—the whole Christ, head and members— discloses the relationship between sexuality's ultimate final end and its intermediate goal here below. (See von Balthasar, "The Meaning of Celibacy," n37). This observation leads us to see the need to relate the treatment of Christ's virginity in eschatology with the consideration of that theme in theological anthropology.

38. "Brighton Address," 11.

39. St. Thomas Aquinas, *In III Sententiae* 12, 3, 1, 1, 2.

40. On the need for all the elements of priestly formation to offer a view of celibacy that is both coherent and profound, von Balthasar writes, "Dogma, exegesis, pastoral studies must be taught so that discernment is induced and is given a sound basis, which cannot be done in a broad study-plan but must be fostered by frequent and varied approaches. This would demand that professors, rectors and spiritual directors work tougher and in the same spirit; that reasons for priestly celibacy be not merely hung on extraneously, in a superficial manner easily refuted by modern psychology and sociology, but that they be presented

as inseparably bound with the innermost of revelation and faith" ("The Meaning of Celibacy," 321–22).

41. "I would like to offer here one very eloquent voice from the Church's tradition that testifies to the fire which burns in the virginal heart of Christ. When St. Mechtilde of Magdeburg talks about the ardor of Christ's love on the cross, she puts it this way: '[Christ's] noble nuptial bed was the very hard Cross on which he leaped with more joy and ardor than a delighted bridegroom'" ("Brighton Address," 14.)

42. Von Balthasar, "The Meaning of Celibacy," 323.

43. Ibid., 328.

6: The Fatherhood of the Celibate Priest

1. Mark 10:24; John 13:33; John 21:5; and Mark 2:5.

2. Cf. Luke 20:38 and Mark 12:27.

3. Joseph Ratzinger, *Introduction to Christianity*, trans. J. R. Foster (San Francisco: Ignatius Press Communio Books, 1990), 197.

4. St. Thomas Aquinas, *Summa Theologiae* II-II.152.2.

5. Second Vatican Council, *Lumen gentium*, n. 42.

6. Second Vatican Council, *Presbyterorum Ordinis*, n. 16.

7. Pope Pius XII, *Menti Nostrae*, n. 20.

7: Beloved Disciples at the Table of the Lord

1. Benedicta Ward, S.L.G., *The Sayings of the Desert Fathers* (Kalamazoo, MI: Cistercian Publications, 1984), 7.

2. Joseph Ratzinger, Pope Benedict XVI, *Jesus of Nazareth: From the Baptism in the Jordan to the Transfiguration* (San Francisco: Ignatius Press, 2008), 49.

3. C. S. Lewis, *The Abolition of Man* (New York: HarperCollins, 2000), 81.

4. See Segundo Galilea, *Temptation and Discernment* (Washington, DC: ICS Publications, 1996), 77–80.

5. Quoted in Paul Murray, *Door into the Sacred: A Meditation on the Hail Mary* (London: Darton, Longman and Todd, 2010), 48–49.

6. Robert Barron, *Catholicism: A Journey to the Heart of the Faith* (New York: Image Books, 2001), 15–19.

7. Charlotte Barr, *Sister Woman* (Cleveland, TN: Parson's Porch Books, 2011), 3.

8: A Recent Study of Celibacy and the Priesthood

1. For a more complete discussion of these findings on priestly happiness, see Rossetti, *Why Priests Are Happy.*

2. Garret Condon, "Priests (Mostly) Happy, Survey Says," *Hartford Courant*, January 19, 2003, http://articles.courant.com.

3. These studies are all referenced in Rossetti, *Why Priests Are Happy*, 87–88.

4. Daniel K. Mroczek and Christian M. Kolarz, "The Effect of Age on Positive and Negative Affect: A Developmental Perspective on Happiness," *Journal of Personality and Social Psychology* 75, no. 5 (1998): 1335.

5. Jeanna Bryner, "Survey Reveals Most Satisfying Jobs," Live Science, April 17, 2007, http://www.livescience.com.

6. Gretchen Anderson, "Loneliness among Older Adults: A National Survey of Adults 45+," AARP "Surveys and Statistics," September 2010, http://www.aarp.org/.

7. Miller McPherson, Lynn Smith-Lovin, and Matthew E. Brashears, "Social Isolation in America: Changes in Core Discussion Networks over Two Decades," *American Sociological Review* 71, no. 353 (June 2006): 358. http://sites.duke.edu/theatrst130s02s2011mg3/files/2011/05/McPherson-et-al-Soc-Isolation-2006.pdf.

8. All correlations reported in this chapter are statistically significant at p < 001.

9. Rossetti, *Why Priests Are Happy*, 219–21.

10. Ibid.

11. Ibid., 223, 226–27.

12. Ibid., 222.

Contributors

REV. RANIERO CANTALAMESSA, O.F.M. CAP., is a priest in the Order of Friars Minor Capuchin. He has served as the Preacher to the Papal Household since 1980, under both Pope John Paul II and Pope Benedict XVI. In this capacity he preaches a weekly sermon in Advent and Lent in the presence of the pope, the cardinals, bishops and prelates of the Roman Curia, and the general superiors of religious orders.

REV. CARTER H. GRIFFIN, STD, is a priest of the Archdiocese of Washington and Vice-Rector of Blessed John Paul II Seminary. He also serves as Vocations Director for the archdiocese.

MARY HEALY, STD, is Associate Professor of Sacred Scripture at Sacred Heart Major Seminary. She is general editor (with Dr. Peter Williamson) of the *Catholic Commentary on Sacred Scripture*, and is author of the first volume, *The Gospel of Mark* (2008).

REV. MSGR. MICHAEL HEINTZ, PHD, is a priest with the Diocese of Fort Wayne-South Bend and rector of St. Matthew Cathedral in South Bend. He is director of the Master of Divinity Program at the University of Notre Dame.

REV. JOSEPH T. LIENHARD, S.J., is Professor of Theology at Fordham University and editor of *Traditio*. From 1975 to 1990 he taught at Marquette University in Milwaukee. He has also held chairs or visiting appointments at John Carroll University, Boston College, St. Joseph's Seminary Dunwoodie, the Pontifical Biblical Institute, and the Pontifical Gregorian University.

REV. MSGR. STEPHEN J. ROSSETTI, PHD, DMIN, is Clinical Associate Professor and Associate Dean for Seminary and Ministerial Programs at the Catholic University of America. A priest of the Diocese of Syracuse, he served as president and CEO of Saint Luke Institute in Silver Spring, Maryland.

THE MOST REVEREND J. PETER SARTAIN was appointed Archbishop of Seattle in 2010. He had previously served as Bishop of Little Rock, Arkansas, from 2000 to 2006 and then as Bishop of Joliet, Illinois, for four years. In 2012 he was elected secretary of the United States Conference of Catholic Bishops for a three-year term.

THE MOST REVEREND ALLEN VIGNERON was appointed Archbishop of Detroit in 2009. Prior to that he was Bishop of Oakland, California, where he oversaw the design and construction of a new cathedral. He served as rector of Sacred Heart Major Seminary from 1994 to 2003.

JOHN C. CAVADINI is the McGrath-Cavadini Director of the Institute for Church Life at the University of Notre Dame. A member of Notre Dame's department of theology, Cavadini served as chair of the department from 1997 to 2010, during which time he led the department to a top-ten position in the National Research Council rankings of doctoral programs. He is an expert in patristic and early medieval theology, with a special focus on the theology of St. Augustine. In November 2009 he was appointed by Pope Benedict XVI to a five-year term on the International Theological Commission.

THE INSTITUTE FOR CHURCH LIFE of the University of Notre Dame exists as an integral component of the university's larger mission of teaching, research, and service to society and the Church. Through its resources, projects, and affiliate centers the Institute reaches out to the whole spectrum of Church leaders—its bishops, clergy, religious, and laity—to provide training and service as well as opportunities for spiritual rejuvenation and personal growth.